MIRACLES
HAPPEN
WHEN
WOMEN
PRAY

JOY HANEY

Miracles Happen When Women Pray
by Joy Haney

Copyright © 1999 by Radiant Life Publications
Stockton, California

Unless otherwise noted all Scripture quotation are from The King James Version of the Bible

Printed in the United States of America
ISBN # 1-880969-35-1

ACKNOWLEDGMENTS

Grateful acknowledgment is made to the following who have granted permission to include the copyrighted selections in this book:

Author Mary Wallace, for "Back Surgery—God's Way" by Richard M. Davis as told to Mary H. Wallace; "Nine Machines and God" by LaJoyce Martin as told to Mary H. Wallace.

Special thanks to the following people:

Carol Rash, Yolanda Lopez, Rev. Steve Cooley and Grace Ann Gee for sharing their stories.
Kim Haney for the cover design.
Kenneth Haney for his encouragement and support.
To all the women everywhere that I have met in my travels who have asked for a book such as this, thank you for being the *lift* to my spirit and encouraging me to keep writing. Your kind words are appreciated.

TABLE OF CONTENTS

INTRODUCTION

On December 16, 1998, I received the following e-mail request from Anna Trujillo and Camila Amador of Michigan:

> We are really interested in seeing more on the internet regarding your ladies' prayer meeting. How are your prayer meetings conducted? What is your focus and what are your goals for your prayer meeting? How is spiritual warfare conducted? What are the results? Is it more of intercessory prayer? Is it more like prayer and share? Is it more like focused prayer? How do you get one started? Great idea for a book so that other churches can start these awesome prayer meetings..."

I printed out this request and laid it aside, mulling it over. In my heart I knew that God was asking me to share with others what I knew. This book is a direct result of that request.

Another e-mail was sent to me while working on this book. It was a confirmation that the book was needed, as you will see in the following letter:

Dear Mrs. Haney,
I just want to take the time out to thank you for your ministry and for your prayers that you pray for the

people over the radio. I am going through a divorce right now, not one that I wanted, but my husband has been having an affair for quite some time, and I would like to believe for restoration. I just don't think I have the faith because my husband is pushing this divorce so hard. Your morning broadcasts help me everyday. You always have something I need for that day. I would very much like to go to your prayer group if I may. I live in Manteca, but I would be willing to travel as far as I need to. I am currently in a church in Modesto, but they don't have a prayer group. Thank you again.

Name withheld

PREFACE

President of the United States of America, Theodore Roosevelt, made the following statement: "Praying mothers are America's greatest assets." [1]

If America had more praying mothers, there would be less crime, violence, hate and torn families.

This book is a cry, a challenge for women in every city of the world to band together and pray. Pray for your family, pray for yourself, pray for your church, pray for your community, pray for your government, pray for the world. Pray, pray, pray.

We are promised that God will hear the prayers of His people. Jeremiah 29:12-14 says, "Then shall ye call upon me and ye shall go and pray unto me, and I will hearken unto you. And ye shall seek me, and find me, when ye shall search for me with all your heart. And I will be found of you, saith the Lord."

II Chronicles 7:14 promises, "If my people, which are called by my name, shall humble themselves, and pray, and seek my face, and turn from their wicked ways; then will I hear from heaven, and will forgive their sin, and will heal their land."

It is time to pray! "With every possible guile that he knows, the devil would snatch us from the closet of prayer. For in prayer man is linked with God, and in that union Satan is baffled and beaten. Prayer is our secret weapon." [2]

FOREWORD

It has been my privilege and honor to be involved in the women's prayer at Christian Life Center under the direction of Joy Haney. Joy is a busy pastor's wife with a large congregation to care for, but the most important thing is that she lives a life of prayer daily. She truly is a woman of prayer and faith!

For the past several years, she has been a real inspiration to many women, not only in Stockton, but around the world. She speaks weekly on Wednesday to those attending the women's prayer meeting known as the *Shepherd's Circle of Prayer*, and also hosts an hour of "live" prayer on Wednesday on KCJH Radio, which consists of a network of twelve stations and translators. Her daily devotion, *Diamonds for Dusty Roads*, is heard Monday through Friday on the same stations.

When we started attending Christian Life Center, I needed a total spiritual restoration, which I found through the women's prayer group. That hour of prayer began to make a real change in my spiritual walk with God. Joy Haney was a true example of a godly woman. Through her prayer and fasting you can see the power she has with God and the faith she demonstrates! God is using her to be a "Crusader of Prayer" for Him across this nation and around the world.

"Crusader of Prayer" for Him across this nation and around the world.

In October 1991, KCJH was raising its yearly budget over a period of three days. During this time, the morning host, Sherrie Woodward, received a phone call from a group in Sacramento, claiming they were praying and fasting against the sharathon in hopes that the station would have to close down. Sherrie recognized this as the work of Satan and asked the listeners to pray against it. As a result of all the prayer, the power of the Lord came mightily into the station and Satan was defeated!

People called in for prayer and started coming by the station to be prayed for. The halls began to fill with those needing healing and salvation. A mighty work of God was started that day. As a result of this outpouring of God's spirit and a need for people to be able to call in their prayer requests, the "Ladies Hour of Prayer" was born. Each Wednesday from 10:00-11:00 a.m., Joy Haney hosts this program. During this hour, over a hundred prayer requests are called in, faxed or e-mailed to the station. Praise reports are also sent in to be read over the air.

Needless to say, Wednesdays are the highlight of my week. Whatever the situation is in my life, things become wonderful when I walk into the prayer room and hear the women praying and I feel the awesome presence of the Lord. After leaving this prayer meeting, we walk across the street to an hour of prayer on the radio. We have prayed for a variety of things, but it is always exciting to read the praise reports. Sometimes we get praise reports for the same prayers we have prayed that very day. It is exhilarating to know the power of prayer.

This book, *Miracles Happen When Women Pray* is GREAT!! One of Joy's statements in the book is as follows:

> When women begin to pray and touch God, they break out of the mold. They do not respond to their situation in a normal way. Instead, they begin to take authority and cast down strongholds which are not rooted in God...Women who know their God and pray specific prayers begin to *dance on top of their problem,* because they...know whom they believe."

When I read this, I wanted to shout, "YES"!!! This is what learning to pray and being specific in my prayers has done for me. Joy Haney will encourage you to *break out of the mold* and *dance on top of your problems* because you will know whom you believe! She has a reckless, contagious faith.

This book shows the importance of women praying. Whether you are just learning to pray, or want to start a prayer meeting or just want to be more effective in your prayer, you will be greatly blessed by *Miracles Happen When Women Pray.* May you too, learn to dance on top of your problems!

Donna Hogue
Prayer Leader

We had just come through a terrible trial. It affected so many areas of my life and I felt dry in my soul. It was then that the Lord directed me to Women's Prayer. The first time there, I could hardly pray for all the crying, but when I got back home, I felt better. My husband saw the change in me and let me go back one day a week. God began to restore and strengthen me.

I learned how to pray effectively, and in time became one of the leaders of the prayer groups. I was constantly growing in God. Good changes were also occurring in my home as I opened my heart and life to Jesus Christ.

During this time, the Lord gave me a dream that KCJH Radio would be giving me a job. It came to pass. One day the morning host, Sherrie Woodward, asked me to oversee the organization and filing of the prayer requests that the station received for the prayer hour with host Joy Haney. I have been doing that job for about six years and it has been wonderful.

Early on we found there was no way we could pray for all the requests in one hour, so when the time was up, we still had prayer requests to pray for. The Lord brought women together to pray for all these requests. The women He chose were intercessors, powerful women of prayer. The more time we spent in the prayer room with the Lord Jesus, the more we grew. Our spiritual gifts developed and our power increased, as well as our love for one another. We became more than friends; we became a team working together for Christ.

I grew so much during this time. Being in the presence of Christ so often and for several hours allowed Him to get

Him to get to the deep issues of my life. What a privilege to pray with Joy Haney and all the other women who have grown dear to me through this time of fellowship with Christ.

The Lord also gave us joy. We often feel like laughing, praising and leaping! He has given us liberty and set us free. I've grown so much these last eight years in the prayer room. God is phenomenal! My home life is so blessed. My husband is blessed. My children are blessed and I am sooooo blessed!

Darlene Malcolm
Prayer Leader

In May 1995, I began to zero in on prayer for my daughter who lived in a foreign land hostile to Christians. I found in God's Word that prayer by more than one person is greater in strength. Deuteronomy 32:30 indicates that with God one could chase a thousand, but two could put ten thousand to flight. With these thoughts in mind, I heard the announcement about the prayer meeting hosted by Joy Haney, and decided I needed to enlist more people to pray for our daughter. So I went to one of the meetings and have been faithful to them ever since.

God began to deal with me on personal issues and others would pray with me. I could feel a transformation of my old ways. Things that were not pleasing to God started to melt away and there came an acceleration of knowledge, understanding, wisdom in His Word and spiritual warfare. I began to see the fruit of our prayers take place.

Another thing that happened was that we learned to allow each other's spiritual gifts to operate in harmony as we ministered to the needs of others. Testimonies were pouring in each week of healings, deliverances and restoration of broken relationships. Prophecies were spoken and came to pass. Many times we felt the birthing of future events. The prayer room was a hospital for the wounded in heart and spirit.

I found out that God's purpose and heartbeat was His relationship with His people, and the relationship of His people with each other. We cannot live alone; we need each other with God at the helm of our hearts.

It is always warm and uplifting in spirit during Wednesday prayer. I'm thankful for it. If I had not been involved in women's prayer and interacted with my sisters in the Lord, I would not have had such wonderful experiences. Thank you, Jesus. Thank you, Sister Joy Haney.

Pam Zeno
Prayer Leader

"I believe it is impossible to live well without prayer, and that prayer is the necessary condition of a good, peaceful, and happy life. The Gospels indicate how one should pray, and what prayer should consist of."

Leo Tolstoy [1]

1

Does God Hear and Answer Women's Prayers?

The word *woman* was coined by God Himself. A minister once said a woman was man's other self.

> And the Lord God said, It is not good that the man should be alone; I will make him an help meet for him. And the Lord God caused a deep sleep to fall upon Adam, and he slept: and he took one of his ribs, and closed up the flesh instead thereof; And the rib, which the Lord God had taken from man, made he a woman, and brought her unto the man (Genesis 2:18,21-22).

The following comments by Matthew Henry on the creation of Eve is most expressive:

If man is the head, she [woman] is the crown, a crown to her husband, the crown of the visible creation. The man was dust refined, but the woman was double-refined, one remove further from the earth...The woman was made of a rib out of the side of Adam; not made out of his head to rule over him, nor out of his feet to be trampled upon by him, but out of his side to be equal with him, under his arm to be protected, and near his heart to be beloved. [2]

The words *woman* and *women* appear over 200 times in the Bible. Women are a force to be reckoned with. They have influence—a very strong influence on those around them. I have often said, "As go the women, so goes the nation."

In the following discourse, Dr. Herbert Lockyer shows how Christ liberated women from being only a mere piece of property for men to dominate, into women of power:

The position of women in Israel was in marked contrast with her status in surrounding heathen nations. Israelite law was designed to protect woman's weakness, safeguard her rights, and preserve her freedom. Under divine law her liberties were greater, her tasks more varied and important, and her social standing more respectful and commanding than that of her heathen sister. The Bible has preserved the memory of women whose wisdom, skill and dignity it willingly acknowledged.

It is from the teaching of our Lord, as well as from His example, that we gather the original function of woman and the obligation of purity toward her. What an understanding of, and sympathy with, women He manifested!...With the coming of Christ a new era dawned for womanhood, and wherever He is exalted woman comes into her own. From the outset of His sojourn on the earth, women were intuitively responsive to His teachings and devoted to His person.

Through the examples of Jesus in His attitude toward women, and as the result of the truth He taught, women were prominent in the activities of the Early Church...That they were among the most conspicuous examples of the transforming power of Christianity is manifest from the admiration and astonishment of the pagan Libanius who exclaimed, "What women these Christians have!" [3]

One of those women was Anna, a prophetess. She was married for only seven years before her husband died, leaving her a widow for 84 years. She chose to live in the temple, giving herself to fastings and prayers day and night. One thing she prayed for was to see the Messiah. This prayer was answered. Before she died she was privileged to see the Christ-child.

When Jesus grew up and began to teach and do miracles, He was sought after by many. He needed a place to rest and get away from the crowd. He found it in the house of Lazarus, who had two sisters, Mary and Martha. While in their home, Jesus spoke His approval of Mary, but gently rebuked Martha. The following passage in Luke 10:38-42 tells the story:

> Now it came to pass, as they went, that he [Jesus] entered into a certain village: and a certain woman named Martha received him into her house. And she had a sister called Mary, which also sat at Jesus' feet, and heard his word. But Martha was cumbered about much serving, and came to him, and said, Lord, dost thou not care that my sister hath left me to serve alone? bid her therefore that she help me. And Jesus answered and said unto her, Martha, Martha, thou art careful and troubled about many things; But one thing is needful: and Mary hath chosen that good part, which shall not be taken away from her.

In essence, the food would be consumed and gone. The dishes would be washed, dried and put away to be used for yet another meal. The housework would be done, the shopping taken care of, the needs of the guests looked after—all these things were important. However, there was something more important.

Someone else can always clean a woman's house, someone else can cook the meals, someone else can serve the guests, but no one can take a woman's place reserved especially for her. That is to sit at the Lord's feet and learn of Him or minister to Him.

Jesus always took time to minister to women who were in need, and also gave approval to women who ministered to Him. The story is told about a woman who had an

"...alabaster box of ointment of spikenard very precious; and she brake the box, and poured it on his head" (Mark 14:3).

Some of the men in the room were indignant towards her and criticized her actions.

> And Jesus said, Let her alone; why trouble ye her? she hath wrought a good work on me...She hath done what she could...Verily I say unto you, Wheresoever this gospel shall be preached throughout the whole world, this also that she hath done shall be spoken of for a memorial of her" (Mark 14:6-7, 9).

Jesus wanted this story to be told in this generation. He wanted it to speak a message to the women. He did not turn her away 2,000 years ago, and He will not turn women away today.

Jesus came to the earth so that everyone could be saved from their sins. Once He walked into the temple, found the passage that had been written by Isaiah and read, "The Spirit of the Lord is upon me, because he hath anointed me to preach the gospel to the poor; he hath sent me to heal the brokenhearted, to preach deliverance to the captives, and recovering of sight to the blind, to set at liberty them that are bruised" (Luke 4:18).

He came to save, heal, deliver and liberate! Jesus is also the high priest for all mankind: men, women and children.

Seeing then that we have a great high priest, that is passed into the heavens, Jesus the Son of God, let us hold fast our profession. For we have not an high priest which cannot be touched with the feeling of our infirmities; but was in all points tempted like as we are, yet without sin. Let us therefore come boldly unto the throne of grace, that we may obtain mercy, and find grace to help in time of need (Hebrews 4:14-16).

Women are included in the invitation to come to the throne of grace and pray. While Jesus was on earth, He ministered to all. John records this phrase, "And he must needs go through Samaria" (John 4:4). Why? There was a woman who needed to be set free from her debilitating lifestyle. She needed to hear about the coming gift of the Spirit.

When Jesus met the woman at Jacob's well, He asked her for a drink. She questioned Him, asking if He knew that she was a Samaritan, for Jews did not talk to Samaritans. Jesus answered her, "If thou knewest the gift of God, and who it is that saith to thee, Give me to drink; thou wouldest have asked of him, and he would have given thee living water" (John 4:10).

The woman could not understand what He was talking about and voiced her doubts. "Jesus answered and said unto her, Whosoever drinketh of this water shall thirst again: But *whosoever* drinketh of the water that I shall give him shall never thirst; but the water that I shall give him shall be in him a well of water springing up into everlasting life" (John 4:13-14).

It was Jesus talking to a woman about spiritual matters. He was revealing to her great truths that would influence all the generations to come. She responded to His ministrations and ran into the city and told the men, "Come, see a man, which told me all things that ever I did: is not this the Christ?" (John 4:29). *She became a woman with a message.*

The Spirit of God is still ministering to women today. He reveals truths to them, He talks with them and sends them forth with a message to anyone who will listen. His instructions on prayer contained the phrase, *every one that asketh.* That includes the women. They *can* have their prayers answered. They *can* walk boldly into the Throne room with authority. They were promised the following:

> Ask, and it shall be given you; seek, and ye shall find; knock, and it shall be opened unto you: For *every one* that asketh receiveth; and he that seeketh findeth; and to him that knocketh it shall be opened...how much more shall your Father which is in heaven give good things to *them* that ask him?" (Matthew 7:7,11).

GOD ANSWERED THE PRAYERS OF WOMEN IN BIBLE TIMES

Hannah

Hannah was the favorite wife of Elkanah, a Levite of Ramathaim Zophim who belonged to one of the most honorable families of the priestly portion of Jacob's descendants the Kohathites. Although a godly man,

Elkanah followed the common custom of polygamy. Elkanah's second wife, Peninnah, caused Hannah much sorrow because of her cruel and jealous tongue.

Hannah was childless and yearned more than anything to have a baby. As the years went by her agony became more intense, and because of Peninnah who mocked and tantalized her, her barrenness grew heavy within her. The fact that Elkanah loved Hannah more, and gave her more than he did Peninnah, only added more fuel to the fire of contempt in Peninnah's heart.

Though Hannah was childless, she was not prayerless. When the family went into the city for their yearly visit to worship and to sacrifice unto the Lord in Shiloh, Hannah did something about her condition. As they were sitting around the table, Peninnah provoked her, causing her to weep. Hannah stood up, pushed her plate back, and went into the temple.

She was in bitterness of soul. She cried and cried and asked God to help her. She said, "O Lord of hosts, if thou wilt indeed look on the affliction of thine handmaid, and remember me, and not forget thine handmaid, but wilt give unto thine handmaid a man child, then I will give him unto the Lord all the days of his life" (I Samuel 1:11).

The priest watched her, because although she was praying desperately, no sound was coming from her lips. He thought she was drunk and accused her of it. Hannah answered, "No, my lord, I am a woman of a sorrowful spirit: I have drunk neither wine nor strong drink, but have poured out my soul before the Lord" (I Samuel 1:15).

Eli, the priest, spoke to her, "Go in peace: and the God of Israel grant thee thy petition that thou hast asked of him" (I Samuel 1:17).

About a year later, God answered her prayer and Samuel was born. When he was just a young child, Hannah kept her promise and took Samuel to the temple to live. Her son became a great prophet and priest of the Lord who influenced many people toward righteousness.

Esther

Esther was an orphan girl who became a Persian queen. She was the daughter of Abihail who lived at Shushan, the Persian royal city. Her family, carried away captive with Jeremiah in about 600 B.C., preferred to remain in the land of captivity rather than return to Jerusalem. When Esther's parents died she came under the guardian care of Mordecai, a palace official, to whom she was related by marriage.

In the third year of the reign of King Ahasuerus, he made a feast unto all his princes, the power of Persia and Media, as well as his nobles and servants. On the seventh day, when the heart of the king was merry with wine, he commanded seven chamberlains to bring Vashti the queen before him with the crown royal in order to show the people her beauty, but the queen refused to come. This enraged the king, so he dismissed her.

This resulted in the need for the king to choose a new queen. For twelve months, the fair maidens prepared themselves for the climatic choosing a new queen. When Esther walked before the king, his heart was smitten by her beauty, and he chose Esther to replace Vashti.

Not long after becoming queen, Esther found out something that caused her to be exceedingly grieved. It was told to her by her maids and chamberlains that Haman, the chief court favorite, had conceived a plan to massacre all the Jews. The king had given Haman his ring and blessings. Notices were placed throughout Shushan about the coming death to the Jews, and there was great mourning and weeping throughout the province. Of course, neither Haman or King Ahasuerus knew that Queen Esther was Jewish.

Upon the instruction of her Uncle Mordecai, Esther fasted three days and prayed to God for her people to be delivered from destruction. Her message to the Jews was:

> Go, gather together all the Jews that are present in Shushan, and fast ye for me, and neither eat nor drink three days, night or day: I also and my maidens will fast likewise; and so will I go in unto the king, which is not according to the law: and if I perish, I perish" (Esther 4:16).

She had to go before the king and ask for an audience with him to reveal her plan to help the Jews. This could have resulted in death if the king had not stretched forth his scepter, indicating that he accepted Esther's approach toward his throne.

After the queen revealed Haman's diabolical plan to the king, he gave orders to have Haman killed. He also ordered that the Jews were to be protected from the heinous crime concocted by the wicked Haman.

What was the result of Esther's answered prayers?

"The Jews had light, and gladness, and joy, and honour. And in every province, and in every city, whithersoever the king's commandment and his decree came, the Jews had joy and gladness, a feast and a good day" (Esther 8:16-17).

God used a woman to deliver His people and to put a stop to the horrendous massacre planned by one warped man, but the deliverance came *after* the prayers were prayed.

Deborah

Deborah is considered to be one of the wisest of all the Old Testament women. The wife of Lapidoth, she was a prophetess, a judge of Israel, a warrior and a poetess. She had the ability to rouse people from their lethargic state into taking action concerning deplorable conditions in the land. She walked with God and interceded for the needs of the people. It was Deborah who prophesied the death of Sisera—not only his death, but how and when it would take place.

She told the mighty warrior Barak, that "...The Lord shall sell Sisera into the hand of a woman" (Judges 4:9). "And Deborah said unto Barak, Up; for this is the day in which the Lord hath delivered Sisera into thine hand" (Judges 4:14).

It was a woman named Jael who went out to meet Sisera and invite him to hide in her tent when he was fleeing from the battle. She gave him a bottle of milk to drink. Then as he laid down to sleep on the floor of the tent, he asked her to stand guard and tell anyone that was looking for him that he was not there.

After he had fallen asleep, "Then Jael Heber's wife took a nail of the tent, and took an hammer in her hand, and went softly unto him, and smote the nail into his temples, and fastened it into the ground: for he was fast asleep and weary. So he died" (Judges 4:21).

Shortly after, Barak came and Jael showed him the enemy who had been killed. It was Sisera, the captain of Jabin's army. So God subdued on that day Jabin the king of Canaan before the children of Israel.

Barak, the warrior, respected Deborah and knew that she had heard from God. It had happened just as she had prophesied. God used a women's prayerful influence and wisdom to help win the battle!

The Syrophenician Woman

A woman of Canaan came to Jesus and cried to Him, "O Lord, thou son of David; my daughter is grievously vexed with a devil" (Matthew 15:22). Jesus did not even answer her and the disciples wanted to send her away. "But she came and worshipped him, saying, Lord, help me" (Matthew 15:25).

Jesus told her it was not time for the Gentiles yet, that He could not do for her what was meant for the Jews. He likened the Jews to children and her to a dog. She did not let that deter her. She simply said, "Truth, Lord: yet the dogs eat of the crumbs which fall from their masters' table" (Matthew 15:27).

Jesus was astonished! Here was a woman who was not a Jew, asking for a miracle. Jesus first of all ignored her, but she kept asking. Secondly, Jesus told her that the door was not open to the Gentiles yet, and that it would not be right to cross over those boundaries. Then He reminded her that her race was known as the *dogs*. Nothing stopped the woman. She was desperate and she always had an answer for Jesus when He made a negative statement about her situation. Finally it happened—that which she had prayed for occurred.

"Then Jesus answered and said unto her, O woman, great is thy faith: be it unto thee even as thou wilt. And her daughter was made whole from that very hour" (Matthew 15:27-28). She received her answer, simply because her desperation would not take *no* for an answer!

GOD HAS ANSWERED THE PRAYERS OF WOMEN IN THE LAST TWO CENTURIES

Colonel Gracie's wife prayed for her husband who was on the Titanic.

With so much interest lately in the story of the sinking of the *Titanic,* there is a lesser known story about one of its passengers. An old copy of the "Christian Observer" recorded the following account:

> One Sunday night in April 1912, an American woman was very weary, yet could not sleep because of an oppression of fear. At last she felt a burden of prayer, and with tremendous earnestness began to pray for her husband, then in the mid-Atlantic, homeward bound on the *Titanic.* As the hours went by she could get no assurance, and kept on praying

in an agony, until about five o'clock in the morning when a great peace possessed her, and she slept.

Meanwhile her husband, Colonel Archibald Gracie, was among the doomed hundreds who were trying frantically to launch the lifeboats from the great ship whose vitals had been torn out by an iceberg. He had given up all hope of being saved himself, and was doing his best to help the women and children. He wished that he could get a last message through to his wife, and cried from his heart, "Good-by, my darling." Then as the ship plunged to her watery grave, he was sucked down in the giant whirlpool. Instinctively he began to swim under water, ice cold as it was, crying in his heart.

Suddenly he came to the surface and found himself near an over-turned lifeboat. Along with several others he climbed aboard, and was picked up by another lifeboat, about five in the morning, the very time that peace came to his praying wife! [4]

John Newton's mother prayed for her wicked son to be saved.

The booklet, "Springs in the Valley," relates the following story of how one woman never gave up, but kept praying for her son:

Picture an old woman with a halo of silvered hair—her worn hands busy over a washboard in a room of poverty—praying—for her son John—John who ran away from home in his teens to become a sailor—John of whom it was now reported that he had become a very wicked man—*praying, praying always*, that her son might be of service to God. The mother believed in two things, the power of prayer and the reformation of her son. God answered the prayer by working a miracle in the heart of John Newton.

John Newton became a sailor-preacher. Among the thousands of men and women he brought to Christ was Thomas Scott, cultured, selfish, and self-satisfied. Because of the washtub prayers another miracle was worked, and Thomas Scott used both his pen and voice to lead thousands of unbelieving hearts to Christ, among them a dyspeptic, melancholic young man, William Cowper by name. He, too, was changed and in a moment of inspiration wrote "There is a Fountain Filled With Blood." All this resulted because a mother took God at His Word and prayed that her son's heart might become as white as the soapsuds in the washtub. [5]

John Newton wrote the immortal song, "Amazing Grace," that is sung all over the world. This is because a mother would not give up praying for her son. God heard and answered her prayers.

An unknown mother prayed for her agnostic son.

C.E. Macartney shares the following story about a young man who turned agnostic, but a praying mother would not let him stay that way.

Dr. James McCosh, president of Princeton, had a custom of praying with members of the senior class before he bade them farewell as they went out into the world. When he asked a certain young man to kneel and pray with him, the man responded that he did not believe in God and did not believe in prayer. Hurt and astonished, the president shook hands with him and bade him farewell.

Years afterward, Dr. McCosh was delivering a course of lectures in Cincinnati. Before going to the lecture hall he was sitting in the lobby of the hotel. A man came and sat down beside him. The man then gave the history of the student who had refused to pray with Dr. McCosh, saying that he had advanced to an important post in the schools of Cincinnati, and that everywhere he was sowing the seeds of unbelief and infidelity. "But," the man added, "he has a godly, praying mother, and I believe that in the end she will win."

A year or two later Dr. McCosh was in his study at Princeton when a young man appeared with his wife. He said to Dr. McCosh: "You do not remember me, but I am the student who refused to let you pray with him. I thought that I was an unbeliever, and wherever I could I sowed the seeds of unbelief; but all the time my godly mother was praying for me. Her prayers have won. I am here in Princeton to enter the theological seminary, and before I go I want you to kneel down with me and offer that long-postponed prayer." 6

A mother prayed for the education of her sons.
C.E. Macartney shares the result:

> Early in the [19th] century the minister at Darlington, Pennsylvania, out on his pastoral round, was riding his horse down a country lane. As he drew up before a humble cottage he heard the sound of a woman's voice lifted in earnest prayer. As he listened he heard this widowed mother, with her boys kneeling at her side, earnestly entreating God that he would open a door for the education of these boys, so that they might become good and useful men.
>
> The pastor dismounted and went in to speak with the widow who had prayed so earnestly, and yet with a note of sorrow in her voice. Struck with the alertness of one of these boys and touched by the woman's petitions, he took the boy with him to the old Stone Academy at Darlington, and there gave him the instruction for which his mother had prayed.
>
> That boy, so handicapped in his birth, and for whom there seemed to be no opportunity, influenced more young minds in America in the last century than any other man. He was William McGuffey, the author of the famous *Eclectic Readers*, which had the extraordinary circulation of a hundred million copies. [7]

Women met together to pray against saloons.
In 1873, a group of women at Hillsboro, Ohio, met and prayed and then read the 146th Psalm. Then they prayed

and pleaded with the saloon keepers to give up their business. Church bells tolled simultaneously with the crusade of prayer and persuasion. On the second day one saloon keeper capitulated. He gave his entire stock to the women saying, "Do as you please with it."

At the end of eight days, everyone of the eleven saloons in the town closed. The brewers of Cincinnati offered a $5,000 reward to anyone who would break up the movement. One usually courageous man tried to do so. In four days he threw up his hands and surrendered to the women.

This crusade of prayer and persuasion led to the formation in 1874 of the "Women's Christian Temperance Union."

A grandmother prayed for protection.

One cold winter, many years ago, the people of a certain town were in great trouble. A hostile army was marching down upon them and they had little doubt the cruel soldiers would destroy their homes. In one family there was an aged grandmother. While the others were fearing and worrying, the grandmother was praying that God would protect them, and that He would build a wall of defense round about them.

During the night they heard the tramping of many feet, and other fearful sounds, but no harm came to them. In the morning they found that just beyond the house the drifted snow had built a wall that had kept the soldiers from coming to their home.

"See," said the grandmother, "God did build a wall around us." [8]

"Holy Ann" prayed for water to come forth from a dry well.

In Canada there lived an Irish saint called "Holy Ann." She lived to be one hundred years old. When she was a young girl, she was working in a family for very small wages under a very cruel master and mistress. They made her carry water for a mile up a steep hill. At one time there had been a well dug there; it had gone dry but stood there year after year. One night she was very tired, and she fell on her knees and cried to God. While on her knees she read these words in the book of Isaiah: "I will open...fountains in the midst of valleys: I will make the wilderness a pool of water, and the dry land springs of water. Produce your cause, saith the Lord; bring forth your strong reasons."

These words struck Holy Ann, and she produced her cause before the Lord. She told Him how badly they needed the water and how hard it was for her to carry the water up the steep hill; then she lay down and fell asleep. She had pleaded her cause and brought forth her strong reasons. The next morning early she was seen to take a bucket and start for the well. Someone asked her where she was going, and she replied, "I am going to draw water from the well."

"Why, it is dry," was the answer.

But that did not stop Holy Ann. She knew whom she had believed, and on she went; and, lo and behold, there in the well was 83 feet of pure, cold water, and it was told that the well never did run dry! [9]

Women who pray with faith, believing, have power with God.

GOD IS ANSWERING WOMEN'S PRAYERS NOW

Doretha Cooley prayed for her husband Steve to be delivered from drugs.

In 1988, Doretha Cooley made her way to the women's prayer meeting at Christian Life Center. She asked for the women to join with her and pray for her husband, Steve. He was in prison at the time for burglary and robbery. He had come from a wealthy family, and had brought them much shame. He had a $300.00-a-day cocaine and heroin habit and was considered to be mean, rough and wild. He had been in prison off and on ever since 1971. In fact, during the 80's he was in Vacaville in the same prison as Charles Manson. Over the years he committed 2,000 crimes to sustain his drug habit. Because of his habit, he suffered two collapsed veins.

Steve eventually received an eight-year sentence. That is when we began to pray for his deliverance and salvation. It was not long until God began to deal with him. Shaking with great conviction, Steve gave his heart to the Lord in Deuel Vocational Institute in Tracy, California. After being filled with the Holy Spirit, his whole life changed. He no longer had any drug addiction and no longer wanted to rob and run wild. The Spirit had tamed his unruly spirit. He started a ministry in the prison and after four years, the Lord did another miracle. He was released from prison January 14, 1992. The officials told him, "You'll be back." He told them, "Yes, I'll be back, but I'll be back wearing a suit and carrying a Bible in my hand." They put him on close supervision because he was a repeat offender, and in the past he had never been successful when put back on the streets. After one year, he was discharged from his parole, and he did not have to finish the rest of his four-year sentence.

After leaving prison, God began to strengthen Steve and Doretha's marriage, and he began to study the Bible fervently. In December 1993, he was asked to be the preacher at a special youth meeting. God anointed him to preach and he was able to influence many of the young people towards God.

Also in 1993, he was asked to be the pastor of the Christian Life Center Boggs Tract Mission. At this writing he has been pastor for almost six years. He is looked upon with respect and is an outstanding citizen in the community. He was so appreciative to the women who prayed that he gave the prayer group a plaque thanking them for their persistent prayers and unceasing love and support to his wife during the difficult time of her life.

Yolanda Lopez healed

Yolanda Lopez, a member of Christian Life Center, shared this testimony with me:

On December 18, 1998, I had gone to see the doctor because I wasn't feeling well. In prayer that day I felt like God had spoken to me these words: "Everyone that walks with Me has to walk with a crown of thorns upon their head that pricks their heart. But they don't realize that at the end of the valley there's awaiting them a crown of jewels. Suffering brings much pain, but I am there in the midst because I have been in that pathway before."

I went to the doctor's office and they ran several tests and said they would call me. Soon after, I received a phone call saying the doctor wanted to see me. I went back to her office one week later and she said the test results showed a tumor was on my left ovary. It was the size of a quarter and almost an inch thick. She couldn't tell if it was cancerous, but she told me to take some pills to help shrink the tumor.

I remembered what God had spoken to me the week before. I remembered seeing a vision of many people walking down a pathway with crowns of thorns upon their heads, but not noticing the end of the valley was brightness—full of God's glory. They did not notice because they had their heads down. Then God spoke to each of them and said, "Lift up your head for you are a child of the King!"

After the doctor told me what was on the report and gave me those pills, she said, "If it doesn't go down, we'll have to remove it by surgery." I was shocked and as I left her office and started to walk with my head hanging down, God's words rang loud in my ears, "Lift up your head. You are a child of the King!"—which I did, smiling. I told Him, "God I don't want to go through another surgery. First my eyes, then my foot, now this. What am I doing wrong?"

I took the pills for two days and then quit taking them because they were making me sick. Instead I had people pray for me and began to pray myself. On January 7, 1999, I had to go retest to find out if anything had happened to the tumor. Before going to the doctor's office, I was in prayer and really talking with God. I told Him, "I don't want to go through with this surgery, but if You want me to I will. But I'll fight You all the way to the table in prayer, because I really don't want it and because I know You can heal me! You have healed me many times before, so I know You can."

Then He spoke these words to me: "I am more with you than what you think I am, for I am Alpha and Omega. I am He who created the heavens and the earth. I rest not!" He spoke other things to me and as He finished speaking, I lifted up my hands and started praising and thanking Him and just weeping before God. I felt the rush of a warm sensation just take over my body within and I knew He was healing me. It was so strong!"

I went back to the doctor on January 19, 1999, and my doctor handed me the report and said, "Here, you read this." She looked bewildered. As I read the report it said, "No signs of any growth. All levels normal." We were both shocked, but then I remembered the warm sensation that had flooded my body on January 7, and knew that God had healed me!

Carol Rash healed of cancer.

Carol Rash, a member of the faculty of Christian Life College, shares her remarkable story:

In October 1990, I had my regular yearly physical and mammogram. I had barely arrived home when the phone rang and the doctor wanted more x-rays taken. The radiologist told me that he saw a very small spot about the size of a small fingernail, but he assured me that "if" it was malignant, it would be very small and in its earliest stage. He recommended that I see a surgeon to schedule a biopsy.

The biopsy was done in November and the surgeon said the tumor was very small and he would be surprised if it was cancer. However, three days later he called to tell me that he was shocked—the tumor was indeed malignant and he recommended a complete mastectomy. Three times I asked the doctor, "Are you sure?" He answered, "Yes, I'm very sure. Just try to get over the shock of it and I'll see you in my office next week to schedule the surgery."

I plopped down on the couch and began to cry. My husband and daughter came in to find out what the news was. Under the effects of that awful initial shock I said, "It's cancer and I might die." You will not understand my reaction unless you have had *cancer* pronounced on you. My mind was in a whirl, and I remembered several dear friends of mine who had passed away from breast cancer.

Our pastor, Kenneth Haney, called me up for special prayer that next Sunday morning and gave words of encouragement and faith to all the church. After that, I felt much better about everything.

I had no problem making the decision to go ahead and have the surgery because I knew I didn't want to carry this cancer in my body. I was scheduled for a modified radical mastectomy on December 14, but the "small" spot turned out to be a malignant tumor almost five centimeters in size. The oncologist said it was one of the largest breast tumors he had seen. Later, a tumor board agreed that I would need to follow up the surgery with chemotherapy, even though the cancer had not spread to the lymph nodes. I was in stage two of cancer because of the size of the tumor.

That is when the very difficult decision had to be made whether or not to take chemotherapy. For several reasons I had a terrible fear of taking it and really was disturbed over having to make that decision so quickly. I tried to get my husband to make the decision for me, but he was very wise in saying, "I can't make that decision for you, but I will promise you that whatever you decide to do, I will stand totally with you in it. If you take chemotherapy and lose all your hair, and if you are sick all the time, I will still love you. If you decide against it and want to trust the Lord, I will stand with you and nothing more will be said."

So the decision was again put right back on me. We attend a large church in Stockton, California, and I began to ask everybody I felt close to what they would do if they were in my shoes. Would you believe half of the people said they would take it and the other half said they wouldn't? The more people I asked, the more confused I became.

My oncologist was really pressuring me to take chemotherapy and even put pressure on my husband to make me do it. But during that last week before I had to give the doctor an answer, I really got desperate in prayer before the Lord. I cried out to God and said, "Lord, please help me to make the right decision for myself and for Your glory." As I was praying fervently the Lord brought to my mind a story from the Old Testament, which I had not heard or read in a long time. I had to get my Bible and look up the passage, II Samuel 24:10-14, where David had sinned in numbering the children of Israel and God gave him a choice of punishment. He could choose to have seven years of famine in the land, or be chased by his enemies for three months, or to have three days of pestilence in the land by the hand of God. David gave his answer in verse 14 where he said, "I am in a great strait; let us fall now into the hand of the Lord; for his mercies are great; and let me not fall into the hand of man."

When I read that verse I said, "Yes, Lord, that answer is just for me. I choose to fall into Your hands, and even if I die tomorrow, I will be in Your hands." Instantly I received such a peace from the Lord, and called my husband at work and told him that I had made my decision. He agreed that he would stand with me in it and we would trust God together.

I could never say this is the right decision for everyone who is facing this, but for me it was directly from the Lord. I felt such an instant calm over it, and could sleep peacefully for the first time in a week.

I just passed my eight-year mark and have regular checkups yearly. The same oncologist checks me each year, and the last time he said, "Well the tissue looks good and the muscle looks good and those are good signs." I said, "Yes, and I thank the Lord." He looked me straight in the eyes and said, "Yes, thank the Lord."

I am just thanking God each day and giving Him the glory for sparing my life this far. The doctor said I wouldn't need to see him for another two years now. It is wonderful to be *in the hands of God.*

These miracles all occurred because women trusted in God and prayed to Him for help. It is essential that each woman becomes a vessel of honor and a woman of prayer and faith. There is a great need for women to give themselves to the things of the Spirit and not to the things of the flesh. There is much death in the earth—morals are decaying, violence is killing masses of people, marriages are dying, kids are killing one another, governments are dying from corruption—it is time for women to bring life back into a decaying generation.

If women give themselves to the things of the Spirit, then life will spring forth.

> For they that are after the flesh do mind the things of the flesh; but they that are after the Spirit the things of the Spirit. For to be carnally minded is death; but to be spiritually minded is life and peace. For if ye live after the flesh, ye shall die: but if ye through the Spirit do mortify the deeds of the body, ye shall live"(Romans 8:5-6,13).

This is not hard to understand. Paul is simply saying that if women will pray, read the Bible and seek after God, both they and those they influence will have life and peace. But if women will not pray or read the Bible and seek only after vanity and temporal things, then both they and those they influence will die. It is essential that the children of this generation see women who care more about the souls of their children than they do their own social standing. This book is a call to women everywhere to begin to pray like you have never prayed before. There is power in prayer!

Paul wrote in I Corinthians 3:16, "Know ye not that ye are the temple of God, and that the Spirit of God dwelleth in you?" He also spoke of the body as being a house. "For we know that if our earthly house of this tabernacle were dissolved, we have a building of God, and house not made with hands" (II Corinthians 5:1).

Isaiah wrote, "Even them will I bring to my holy mountain, and make them joyful in my house of prayer: their burn-offerings and their sacrifices shall be accepted upon mine altar; for mine house shall be called an house of prayer for all people" (Isaiah 56:7). Jesus quoted this in the temple when He threw out the money changers: "It is written, My house shall be called the house of prayer" (Matthew 21:13).

If each woman is a temple, a house for the Spirit, then that house must be a *house of prayer*. Women were made to pray and commune with the Lord. They are incomplete without prayer. If women do not pray, they throw away power, miracles and great joy. It is time to pray!

"If you do take time for prayer you will have a real, living God, and if you have a living God you will have a radiant life."

R. A. Torrey [1]

2

Why it is Important for Women to Pray Together

Something powerful happens when women pray together. Walls break down, hearts blend together, faith is generated and courage springs forth like a lion. One voice in prayer is powerful, but several voices praying together are like a mighty ocean. Moses expressed the difference between one and two when he said, "...*one* chase[s] a thousand, and *two* put ten thousand to flight..." (Deuteronomy 32:30).

There are many things that happen as a result of fervent prayer. Prayer without fervor has no heart in it; it is empty ritual. However, the fervent prayer of the righteous accomplishes much. Prayer is essential to the human soul. Without prayer, life is barren of all the things God wants to give to His children.

Prayer helps women to learn obedience to God, to be godly and to walk in love. It is good for women to pray together. Jesus said in Matthew what happens when two or three are gathered together:

"Again I say unto you, That if two of you shall agree on earth as touching any thing that they shall ask, it shall be done for them of my Father which is in heaven. For where two or three are gathered together in my name, there am I in the midst of them" (Matthew 18:19-20).

A unified effort has much power. This is proven in the example of the building of the tower of Babel. God had this to say about it: "Behold, the people is one, and they have all one language; and this they begin to do: and now nothing will be restrained from them, which they have imagined to do" (Genesis 11:6). There is power in togetherness!

When women pray together, they are lifted up into the heavenlies. "And hath raised us up together, and made us sit together in heavenly places in Christ Jesus" (Ephesians 2:6). Grudges, resentments, ill-will and suspicion all leave when women pray together. There is a washing, a cleansing, a releasing into a realm of pure love and joy that can be attained only by being in the presence of the Lord God! David said it well in Psalm 16:11: "Thou wilt shew me the path of life: in thy presence is fulness of joy: at thy right hand there are pleasures forevermore."

Following are some of the things that happen as a result of prayer.

PRAYER RELEASES PRESSURE

Dr. Hysloop, a respected psychiatrist, stated the following:

> As one whose whole life has been concerned with the sufferings of the mind, I would state that of all the hygienic measures to counteract disturbed sleep, depression of spirits, and all the miserable sequels of a distressed mind, I would undoubtedly give the *first place* to the simple habit of prayer. [2]

Dr. William S. Sadler, also a psychiatrist, advises physicians how to get at the cause of people's troubles:

> Prayer is a powerful and effectual worry-remover. Men and women who have learned to pray with childlike sincerity, literally talking to, and communing with the Heavenly Father, are in possession of the great secret whereby they can cast their care upon God, knowing that He careth for us. A clear conscience is a great step toward barricading the mind against neuroticism.
>
> Many are victims of fear and worry because they fail properly to maintain their spiritual nutrition....The majority of people liberally feed their bodies, and many make generous provision for their mental nourishment; but the vast majority leave the soul to starve, paying very little attention to their spiritual nutrition; and as a result the spiritual nature is so weakened that it is unable to

exercise the restraining influence over the mind which would enable it to surmount its difficulties and maintain an atmosphere above conflict and despondency. [3]

Dr. Sadler further states that "Prayer is a safety valve for the mind and the soul. If Christianity were practically applied to our everyday life it would so purify and vitalize the race that at least one-half of our sickness and sorrow would disappear." [4]

There is an incident in the New Testament that proves what prayer can do for the emotions. After the miracle by the Gate Beautiful in which a lame man had been healed, the priests and Sadducees forced Peter and John to be put into prison for the night. The next day, Peter and John were brought before the Sanhedrin and told to not speak of the name of Jesus anymore. They threatened Peter and John and told them to keep quiet in the marketplace and to not do any more miracles, or they would be in trouble with the magistrates.

Peter and John had two choices: They could buckle under and keep quiet or they could pray. They chose to pray. They gathered together with those of like faith,

> And when they had prayed; the place was shaken where they were assembled together; and they were all filled with the Holy Ghost, and they spake the word of God with boldness. And with great power gave the apostles witness of the resurrection of the Lord Jesus; and great grace was upon them all" (Acts 4:31,33).

Prayer released the tension and worry caused by the threats of the leaders in power. It not only released them, but power from heaven was released back to them to go forth with new boldness, courage and grace. Prayer is the greatest help in dealing with pressure successfully.

PRAYER CHANGES WOMEN INSIDE

When Hannah went into the temple to pray, she was weeping, bowed down at her wit's end. After prayer, and after hearing a word from the priest, she left encouraged. The Scriptures describe the change: "So the woman went her way, and did eat, and her countenance was no more sad" (I Samuel 1:18).

Was no more sad is a transformation of the soul and mind. Hannah left with hope and was satisfied and happy. She knew that God had heard her prayer and was going to answer it.

Prayer in a crisis changes a timid woman into a strong one. This was proven in the story told in Chapter One about Esther. Before prayer, Esther was afraid. After Mordecai had told her she had to go to the king and make supplication unto him for the Jewish people, she sent the following message to him:

> All the king's servants, and the people of the king's provinces, do know, that whosoever, whether man or woman, shall come unto the king into the inner court, who is not called, there is one law of his to put him to death, except such to whom the king

shall hold out the golden sceptre, that he may live:
but I have not been called to come in unto the king
these thirty days (Esther 4:11).

Mordecai sent back the following word to Esther:

Think not with thyself that thou shalt escape in the
king's house, more than all the Jews. For if thou
altogether holdest thy peace at this time, then shall
there enlargement and deliverance arise to the Jews
from another place; but thou and thy father's house
shall be destroyed: and who knoweth whether thou
art come to the kingdom for such a time as this"
(Esther 4:14).

Mordecai's answer caused Esther to say,

Go, gather together all the Jews that are present in
Shushan, and fast ye for me, and neither eat nor
drink three days, night or day: I also and my
maidens will fast likewise; and so will I go in unto
the king, which [is] not according to the law: and if I
perish, I perish (Esther 4:16).

In other words, "O.K. I'll go into the king, *after* all the
Jews pray, my maidens pray and I pray myself." She knew
the power of prayer and fasting.

Prayer helps define the mission God has for each
woman. It equips her and gives her grit and nerve to do
what needs to be done. Prayer gives them courage. General
Dwight Eisenhower once said, "Prayer gives you courage

to make the decisions you must make in a crisis and then the confidence to leave the result to a Higher Power." [5]

Richard Trench captures the essence of change in the following poem:

"Prevailing Prayer"
Lord, what change within us one short hour
Spent in Thy presence will prevail to make!
What heavy burdens from our bosoms take,
What parched grounds revive as with a shower!
We kneel, and all around us seems to lower;
We rise, and all, the distant and the near,
Stands forth in sunny outline brave and clear;
We kneel, how weak! We rise, how full of power! [6]

PRAYING TOGETHER INCREASES FAITH WITHIN

Charles Spurgeon told the following story:

Some years ago, two men, a bargeman and a coal miner, were in a boat above the rapids of a waterfall, and found themselves unable to manage it, being carried so swiftly down the current that they must both inevitably be borne down and dashed to pieces. One was saved by grasping a rope that was thrown to him. The same instant that the rope came into his hand, a log floated by the other man. The thoughtless and confused bargeman, instead of seizing the rope, laid hold on the log. It was a fatal mistake; they were both in imminent peril; but the one was drawn to shore, because he had a connection with the people on the land, while the other, clinging to the loose, floating log, was borne irresistibly along, and never heard of afterwards.

This is the way it is with women. Women need to hold on to the rope of faith that is thrown out by other women who have been there and done that! We live in a turbulent generation filled with violence and festered with fear. It is not good for women to live isolated, or keep to themselves and try to make it alone. "For none of us liveth to himself [herself], and no man [woman] dieth to himself [herself]" (Romans 14:7).

It is good to join together and pray about things. When one woman receives an answer to prayer and she shares her answer, it causes hope to be kindled in the heart of the other women who are listening to her praise report.

Faith is contagious! When a group of women get together and begin to pray prayers of faith, talk about the Word of God and encourage one another to believe for a miracle, it is like being inoculated by a serum of faith.

Satan does not like unity in prayer, because it keeps women loving one another, sharing their faith and living in great victory. He is like the lion in the following story:

Aesop tells about four bulls who were great friends. They went every where together, fed together and lay down to rest together, always keeping so close to each other that if any danger were near they could all face it at once.

Now there was a lion which had determined to have them but he could never get at them singly. He was a match for any one alone, but not for all four at once. However, he used to watch for his opportunity, and when one lagged the least bit behind the others as they grazed, he would slink up and whisper that the other bulls had been saying unkind things about him. This he did so often that at last the four friends became uneasy. Each thought the other three were plotting against him. Finally, as there was no trust among them, they went off by themselves, their friendship broken.

That was what the lion wanted. One by one he killed them, and made four good meals.

This is just what Satan wants to do: Keep the women disconnected from one another and from the power line. He wants to destroy their faith in each other, as well as their faith in God.

There is something powerful in the bonding together as one. Women are stronger together than if they are alone. Their faith increases, so that they feel like they can do anything.

In Thebes, Greece, during the time before Christ's birth, there was a small band of three hundred cavalry in the Theban army, who proved a great terror to any enemy with whom they were called to fight. They were companions, who had bound themselves together by a vow of perpetual friendship, determined to stand together until the very last drop of their blood was spilled upon the ground. They were called "The Sacred Battalion," and they were bound alike by affection for the State and fidelity for each other, and thus achieved marvels, some of which seem almost impossible. [7]

Women who pray together have marvelous results and many of their answers seem impossible, but with God, they have found that all things are possible. They choose to believe the words of Jesus: "Only Believe" (Mark 5:36).

PRAYER GIVES STRENGTH AND KEEPS WOMEN CONNECTED TO THE POWER LINE!

Difficult circumstances, crushed dreams, heartbreaking disappointments and constant sorrows can all be lifted if women begin to pray together. They are renewed with new strength to go forward in spite of any. trial.

Jesus equated strength with prayer. He said, "...men [women] ought always to pray, and not to faint" (Luke 18:1). Prayer is nourishment to the soul just as food is nourishment to the body. Prayer is soul food.

Years ago, a delicate little woman, who had obviously seen better days, continued to go to work as a seamstress, although past the traditional threescore and ten years. The daughter of one of the families in which she was employed, marveling at her quiet endurance, asked her one day how she managed to work so hard and so steadily. "Well, my dear," replied the patient voice, "sometimes it seems hard. Often I get up in the morning feeling so weak and faint that it seems impossible to go through the day's work. But, you see, I'm like a tram car before it is connected with the power wire. The first thing I do is to *connect with the Power*. When I have said my prayers, I feel my hand in God's, and the power of His Spirit passing into me, and then I can go on and do what I have to do." [8]

Oliver Wendell Holmes wrote, "Just so sure as you keep drawing out your soul's currency without making new deposits, the next thing will be: 'No funds.' Soul deposits and checks must more than balance if we are to be spiritually dynamic." [9]

"He [God] giveth power to the faint; and to them that have no might he increaseth strength" (Isaiah 40:29). How? "They that wait upon the Lord shall renew their strength; they shall mount up with wings as eagles; they shall run, and not be weary; and they shall walk, and not faint" (Isaiah 40:31).

Someone once said, "Much kneeling keeps us in good standing with God. We cannot stumble when we are on our knees." Prayer gives women power to walk with confidence and victory.

The power comes from surrendering to God. Surrendering one's will to the *divine will* may seem to be a negative procedure, but it gives positive results. Psychologist Wallace Emerson once wrote, "It is a will that, while giving up the mastery, has finally become something of a master in its own house...." [10]

When women begin to pray in humility and open the door so that Christ may occupy the throne room of the soul, it is then that they can experience real living, new strength, fresh vitality and inward peace.

Years ago, Dr. Lena Sadler, a psychiatrist, had asked her husband, Dr. William S. Sadler, also a psychiatrist, to see one of her patients, a refined, highly educated woman. The patient still did not respond, even after their combined psychiatric counselings. Dr. William Sadler advised his wife that she need not expect any worthwhile improvement until her patient's mental life was set in order and numerous psychic slivers were removed. To the question of how long did he think that would take, he replied, "Probably a year or more."

Dr. William Sadler wrote the following account of what happened concerning this patient:

> Imagine my surprise when this patient walked into my office a few days later and informed me that her troubles were all over, that the things she had assured me a few days previously she could never do, had all been done, that everything I had asked her to do as part of her *cure* had been set in operation—she had completely overhauled her social, family, and personal life, had made numerous confessions, and had accomplished a score of almost impossible mental and moral stunts.
>
> In reply to my astonished question, "How in the world did you ever do all this and effect this great change in your mental attitude toward yourself and the world in less than one week?" she smilingly replied, "Dr. Lena taught me to pray." [11]

Women must have contact with God in order to live victoriously over the inner conflicts that life brings. It is the spirit that must be fed and nurtured. This is not done with material things. The Spirit of God is the only thing that will bring true eternal victory and power over oneself. Ralph Waldo Emerson once said, "Great men are they who see that the spiritual is stronger than any material force..." [12]

James Hudson Taylor, who formed the China Inland Mission under great difficulty, wrote the following: "Many Christians estimate difficulties in the light of their own resources, and thus attempt little and often fail in the little they attempt. All God's giants have been weak men who did great things for God because they reckoned on His power and presence with them." 13

Women who pray reckon on His power and presence with them!

A minister was being shown through a large plant where locomotives were built. Pointing at one completed locomotive, the guide said, "This locomotive is the last word in engine building!" The minister exclaimed with admiration, "What a mighty thing!" "Yes," said the guide, "if there are three things attending it. It must have power generated by internal combustion of crude oil. It must be on the rails, for its power would bring destruction if it is derailed. It must have a good engineer, for it will run efficiently only when rightly handled." The minister replied, "That's just like a Christian. We are powerful and useful only when we are filled with the fullness of God, walking in His way, and utterly under the Holy Spirit's control!" 14

The way for women to be filled with His Spirit is to stay connected to Him through prayer!

CONSISTENT PRAYER CHANGES WOMEN INTO RADIANT CHRISTIANS

Joseph Parker wrote the following words:

The morning is the time fixed for my meeting the Lord. This very word morning is as a cluster of rich grapes. Let me crush them, and drink the sacred wine. In the night I have buried yesterday's fatigue, and in the morning I take a new lease of energy. Blessed is the day whose morning is sanctified! Successful is the day whose first victory is won in prayer.

Having communed with the Heavenly Father in the garden of prayer when the dew of blessing awaits at sunrise reminds me of a certain valley in Romania where they grow nothing but roses for the Vienna market. The perfume of that valley in the time of the rose crop is such that if you go into it for a few minutes, wherever you go the rest of the day, people know where you have been. The fragrance goes with you. Meeting Him in the morning causes the fragrance of His presence to go with you throughout the entire day. [15]

When women come into contact with Jesus Christ, they are never the same. He came to liberate them and set them free. When Jesus walked upon the earth, before His ascension into glory, He healed many people. One of those He set free from the dominion of sin was a woman named Mary Magdalene. After her deliverance, she followed Jesus closely.

And it came to pass afterward, that he went throughout every city and village, preaching and shewing the glad tidings of the kingdom of God: and the twelve were with him, And certain women, which had been healed of evil spirits and infirmities, Mary called Magdalene, out of whom went seven devils, And Joanna the wife of Chuza Herod's steward, and Susanna, and many others, which ministered unto him of their substance (Luke 8:1-3).

Notice: *many* women followed Jesus. Notice also, He preached *glad* tidings. He made people glad! He lifted their spirits.

The moment Jesus' compassionate eyes saw the wild-eyed and cringing woman of Magdala, He saw in her the ministering angel who would be a blessing to His own heart and to others. In His authoritative voice He commanded the tormenting demons to come out and stay out of her. "Back! back! to your native hell, ye foul spirits of the pit," and the miracle happened. Her deranged and nerve-racked mind became as tranquil as the troubled lake Jesus calmed. Sanity returned...and she was made whole. Now, "clothed and in her right mind," she was ready to become one of the most devoted woman disciples of Him to whom she owed so much." [16]

She was changed into a radiant disciple. Mary Magdalene became the first evangelist of the resurrection. Jesus told her, "...go to my brethren, and say unto them, I ascend unto my Father, and your Father: and to my God, and your God. Mary Magdalene came and told the disciples that she had seen the Lord, and that he had spoken these things unto her" (John 20:17-18).

' The following story which depicts the radiance of Christ dwelling in and shining through an individual is shared by Mrs. Ruby Miller:

> Many years ago when the great missionary Adoniram Judson was home on furlough, he passed through the city of Stonington, Connecticut. A young boy playing about the wharves at the time of Judson's arrival was struck by the man's appearance. Never before had he seen such a light on any human face. He ran up the street to a minister to ask if he knew who the stranger was. The minister hurried back with him, but became so absorbed in conversation with Judson that he forgot all about the impatient youngster standing near him.

> Many years afterward that boy—who could never get away from the influence of that wonderful face—became a famous preacher named Henry Clay Trumbull. In a book of memoirs he penned a chapter entitled: "What a Boy Saw in the Face of Adoniram Judson." That lighted countenance had changed his life. Even as flowers thrive when they bend to the light, so shining, radiant faces come to those who constantly turn toward Christ! [17]

Author Mrs. Charles E. Cowman tells how to be a radiant woman in the following paragraph:

Spend time in prayer. You cannot be a radiant Christian in any other way. Why is it that prayer in the name of Christ makes one radiantly happy? It is because prayer makes God real. *The gladdest thing upon earth is to have a real God!* You cannot have vital faith in God if you give all your time to the world and to secular affairs, to reading the newspapers and to reading literature, no matter how good it is. [18]

THE CONCENTRATED PRAYER POWER OF WOMEN CAN GO AROUND THE WORLD

Prayer is the greatest communication system between heaven and earth. Prayer knows no boundaries. Many incidents have proven this, one of them being the following story told by Walter B. Knight:

A thrilling incident happened in a little hut in Africa. A missionary awoke suddenly. She had a feeling of imminent danger. Fear held her in a vice-like grip. The moon's rays shone through the window, but she could see nothing wrong. She continued to have a feeling of great danger so she awoke her husband. They talked in a whisper. Looking beside the bed, they saw a fearsome creature—a giant cobra whose head was raised, ready to strike and inject venom into the flesh of the missionaries. Quickly the husband reached for his rifle and shot the cobra through its head.

Our story is not complete. One day while a friend of the missionaries was sweeping the floor in her Canadian town, she had an irresistible urge to pray for these missionaries. "They are right now in great danger," she said to herself. So she began to pray. Presently God's peace came into her heart. She knew that God had worked in behalf of her faraway friends. Later, when the missionaries told her of their frightful experience, she compared the date and time of the two experiences. The peril of the missionaries and the burden to pray for them corresponded to the minute! [19]

Grace Ann Gee of Quebec, Canada, shares in the following story how this concept worked in her family's life:

On December 22, 1987, in Harvey Station, New Brunswick, Canada, after a hectic day of Christmas preparations, our family had all gone to bed. Shortly after midnight, I was awakened by the smell of smoke and then a loud swirling, gushing sound. Throwing my arm across my husband David, I screamed, "Honey, the house is on fire!"

We jumped out of bed and ran to the stairway, but the smoke and heat were so unbearable it was impossible to go downstairs. Fear and panic struck us. Our ten-year-old daughter, Amy Beth, was sleeping on the first floor of our home. We then ran across the hall and grabbed our eight-year-old son,

Chadwick, and rushed to his window, knowing this was our only way out.

My husband dropped our son down first, then he and I both jumped from the second story, all of us in our bed clothes and bare feet. There was a drift of snow to break our fall, so none of us broke any bones. We were on our feet instantly, running to the nearest window and door, hoping one might be unlocked. Every minute counted, knowing that Amy Beth was inside the house in the horrible heat and smoke.

David began to pound on her window and shout her name, trying to use his bare hands to break through. Being desperate, I hailed a truck on the highway in front of our house. The two men later told us they weren't going to stop, thinking it was a marital dispute seeing me in my night gown and bare feet. But one said, "We'd better stop because the lady seems so desperate." They took a shovel and helped my husband break the second pane of glass and a set of grills out of the window.

Thick, black smoke billowed out of the bedroom window. One of the men said, "We can't go in there."

But the love of a father said, "Oh, yes we can. We *have* to go in there." David climbed in the window and found Amy Beth. But when he tried to lift her, he felt himself being overcome by the thick smoke and sickening fumes. Right at that moment he felt a presence and strength help him lift her and hand her out the window to the men waiting outside.

He then managed to climb out himself. When he got to Amy Beth, the only sign of life was a faint moan.

Our whole family was taken to the hospital, but Amy Beth did not regain consciousness until the following day. We feel that her speedy recovery was because of what happened in another city.

In the community of Ripples, New Brunswick, where we had formerly lived, there was an elderly woman who was known to be a mighty prayer warrior. Her name was Violet Flowers. She also was awakened shortly after midnight, feeling a heavy burden for our family, though she did not know what was taking place in our lives. Putting wood in her kitchen stove, she sat in her rocking chair all night long and prayed for us. Her burden of prayer did not lift until mid-afternoon the following day. I credit Amy Beth's complete recovery to her earnest prayers.

I believe with all my heart that God placed angels in the bedroom beside my husband and helped him and Amy Beth to get out of our burning home. He brought us through the fire without a burn or broken bone. What could have been a fatal tragedy was turned into a miracle because someone cared enough to pray for us when they felt a premonition of danger. [20]

It is an amazing thing how *one* woman praying in a certain place can have an effect upon a situation in another location.

IT IS A GOOD THING FOR WOMEN TO DRAW NEAR TO GOD IN PRAYER

"But it is good for me to draw near to God: I have put my trust in the Lord God, that I may declare all thy works" (Psalm 73:28).

Drawing near to God helps shape the character of women. It makes them more Christlike and pure. They become the molders of the children. Their walk, talk and thoughts influence all those with whom they come in contact.

Henry Drummond wrote the following about Christ's influence:

> Nothing could be more simple, more intelligible, more natural, more supernatural. It is an analogy from an everyday fact. Since we are what we are by the impacts of those who surround us, those who surround themselves with the highest will be those who change into the highest. If to live with men, diluted to the millionth degree with the virtue of the Highest, can exalt and purify the nature, what bounds can be set to the influence of Christ?" [21]

Prayer causes women to have the *upward* look. My voice shalt thou hear in the morning, O Lord; in the morning will I direct my prayer unto thee, and I will *look up*" (Psalm 5:3). Women are plagued with many troubles concerning their children, finances, business and relationships. They can look up because in prayer, they gain help, strength and confidence; God becomes their gain help, strength and confidence; God becomes their refuge. "The Lord also will be a refuge for the oppressed, a refuge in times of trouble" (Psalm 9:9).

God is faithful to hear their cry. "And having an high priest over the house of God; Let us draw near with a true heart in full assurance of faith...Let us hold fast the profession of our faith without wavering; (for he is faithful that promised;) (Hebrews 10:21-23).

"Prayer is the nearest approach to God, and the highest enjoyment of Him, that we are capable of in this life. It is the noblest exercise of the soul, the most exalted use of our best faculties, and the highest imitation of the blessed inhabitants of Heaven."

Williama Law [1]

3
How to Begin a Women's Prayer Meeting

Everything starts with a good plan, but before the plan, there must first be a concept and a desire. Someone has to want to have the prayer meeting before it can come into fruition. To have a successful prayer meeting, the women must first of all determine that they will not let anything stop them from attaining their heart's desire.

Desire is not merely a wish; it is a deep-seated craving or intense longing. David expressed it in the 63rd Psalm. "O God, thou art my God; early will I seek thee: my soul thirsteth for thee, my flesh longeth for thee in a dry and thirsty land, where no water is; To see thy power and thy glory" (Psalm 63:1-2).

After the desire, then the plan must evolve. Choose two or three women to get together and discuss the desire and the need for a prayer meeting. Then begin to plan. Do

73

not be afraid to venture forth and do it, because you cannot succeed if you do not try.

> *If you would have some worthwhile plans*
> *You've got to watch your can't's and can's;*
> *You can't aim low and then rise high;*
> *You can't succeed if you don't try;*
> *You can't go wrong and come out right;*
> *You can't love sin and walk in light;*
> *You can't throw time and means away;*
> *And live sublime from day to day.*[2]

You *can* have a successful prayer meeting. The best time to begin is NOW! There are basically four things that need to be chosen to begin a prayer meeting: A location, a leader, a scheduled time, and a name.

A. A room or meeting place
The best place to meet for prayer is at a church, but it needs to be in a specially chosen room. Many churches today have prayer rooms. If your church does not, you need to discuss your desire with your Pastor and reach a decision on location with him.

During the first part of the prayer, it is best if the room is dimly lighted. As the prayer meeting progresses, more light can be made available for the reading of the Word and special prayer.

If you do not have access to a church prayer room, then find another place. The main thing is to gather together to pray. It is not a complicated thing. It can be done if *need* and *desire* are strong enough.

B. A leader

The leader should be a woman full of God's spirit with a genuine love for God, His Word and other people. It is a wonderful thing if the pastor's wife can fill this position, but it is not always possible. Therefore, a godly woman who works well with people, who has wisdom and leadership qualities, can be chosen to fill this important place.

The leader must be able to flow with God's spirit, be sensitive to the needs of others, and have authority to be able to handle a problem if one should arise. She should be a woman of good report, whom others will respect and follow.

If you have no leader, and are not sure who should be the leader, then just begin to pray together. God will cause the leader to emerge or come forth from the group.

C. The time

A time should be made available so that the women who *desire* to pray together are able to attend. Often a good time for prayer is mid-week, in the morning when the children are in school. This brings up two questions: What about the toddlers? What about the women who work outside the home?

These two questions can be answered this way:

1. During the prayer time, utilizing a good daycare could be considered. If that is not financially possible, then baby-sitting can be organized and arranged. Some women prefer to have their children come with them. They spread

a blanket on the floor, put some toys out and often the children are content to play while mother prays.

2. Poll the women who work secular jobs. If there are enough women who *desire* to have a weekly prayer meeting, then an evening can be chosen. Because of the already crowded schedules this can be a problem, but with a little effort and flexibility on everyone's part it can be done. You might consider having both a morning prayer meeting, and an evening one.

D. A name

It is good to have a name for promotional reasons, stability and longevity. Women like to have something that is defined, not a hazy *"maybe we'll meet, maybe we won't"* type of situation. A name allows the women to identify with something permanent.

After a name is chosen, business cards printed with an appropriate logo could be passed out to interested women. The local Christian radio station can do a promo for you. Prospective prayer warriors can be reached through church bulletins and word-of-mouth communication, as well as personal letters.

After the prayer meeting is organized, the following two things need to be considered:

1. Supplies for the prayer room

It is good to have a box of Kleenex available. A round table covered with a nice tablecloth in which to place books on prayer, a Bible, a basket with prayer cloths*, a basket filled with note paper to write prayer needs on, and a small bottle of oil.

*Note: Often people ask for anointed prayer cloths to give to people in the hospitals, in prisons or to people out of town. We base this practice on Acts 19:11-12, when Paul sent out cloths to those who needed healing. "And God wrought special miracles by the hands of Paul. So that from his body were brought unto the sick handkerchiefs or aprons, and the diseases departed from them, and the evil spirits went out of them."

If the prayer room is used by others and is left open 24 hours a day, then often a problem presents itself. Supplies have a way of disappearing. People borrow a book and forget to bring it back, children scribble on the note paper, the Bible is used and is never returned. To alleviate these problems, the women can appoint someone to lock up their supplies between prayer meetings.

2. Decor of the prayer room

I have seen simple prayer rooms and extravagant prayer rooms. Each locale must work with what is available and what is practical for them. The following is a list of suggestions for decor:

a. Maps of the city, the world and special interest maps.

b. Flags which represent the various countries.

c. Pictures of important leaders in the lives of the local Church.

d. Pictures of the missionaries the church is supporting.

e. Prayer areas designated for special prayer— leadership, family, government, etc.

f.   Tables placed in the above areas with prayer
     helps (cards with prayers on them, a globe,
     special chairs, etc.).
g.   Special lighting for designated areas,
     focusing on object of prayer.
h.   Scriptures blown up and artfully framed
     placed at strategic points.
i.   Pictures of people praying.

"Prevailing, or effectual prayer, is that prayer which attains the blessing that it seeks. It is that prayer which effectively moves God. The very idea of effectual prayer is that it affects its object."

Charles G. Finney [1]

4
How to Conduct the Prayer Meeting

There are a variety of ways to conduct a prayer meeting. The type of prayer meeting that is discussed in this chapter has proven to be successful. Hundreds of women have been healed, blessed, changed and uplifted through these times of organized prayer.

PART I: Steps in a Prayer Meeting.

The following steps will help *those who already know how to pray*, conduct a successful prayer meeting. These steps have been practiced successfully in the *Shepherds Circle of Prayer*, in Stockton, California.

Step 1: Individual Supplications

Prayer meetings should be prayer meetings, not gossip sessions. The first woman walks in, kneels down and begins to pray. The second woman does the same. The third woman walks in and begins to pray. Other women follow suit. The lights are dim, soft music is playing, and the sound of prayer begins to crescendo as the voices of women blend together to call upon their God.

When women come together to pray, they all come with full hearts. Some are dealing with personal problems, some with depression or fears; others are dealing with marital, financial or physical problems. When women enter the prayer room it is best if they first find a place to pray where they can share their heart with God. It is not good to enter the prayer room chatting in a light-hearted manner. The reason for the gathering must be remembered: A time set apart to talk to God.

Treat the prayer room with respect. Treat God with respect. Treat each other with respect. When you enter the place of prayer, you have just made an appointment with royalty, the King of kings, and it is a hallowed place.

Each woman begins to pray in her own way about her world. God has the ability to hear everyone pray at the same time. He is not confused, but hears each individual prayer. At the *Shepherd's Circle of Prayer* at Christian Life Center, we encourage the women to articulate their prayers, to pray out loud, to praise the Lord, to talk to Him, to shut out the world and enter into God's presence.

There is nothing quite like having a room filled with women who are pouring their hearts out to God. Psalm 62:8 says, "Trust in him at all times; ye people, *pour* out your heart before him: God is a refuge for us." The intensity, the energy and desperation are felt as tears flow. Cries for help mingle together and burst forth from lips of clay until there is a meeting together of humanity and Divinity.

Step 2: A Call to Worship

When the intensity is lessened, pressures are released and the presence of God has melted the women together in love, the leader, being sensitive to God's leading, can call the women to stand and worship God together.

What power! What glory as women begin to magnify the Lord! As He is exalted among them, there is a shift in the atmosphere. Faith begins to build and hope replaces despair. Faces begin to shine with radiance and light. Something supernatural happens in the prayer room. While the rest of the world continues to plod along in heaviness and doubt, there is genuine power flowing like a river into each woman by the Spirit of the living God. It is the best-kept secret in the world!

The women become filled with light, hope, faith and love. They become empowered with courage, so that they feel as if they can face any situation and win.

Worshipping the Lord is something to get excited about. To think that God in all His glory would condescend to a humble prayer meeting and meet with women who have gathered together to call upon His name is mind-boggling. God deserves the highest form of praise and worship.

Psalm 47:1 gives one way to acknowledge God's greatness: "O clap your hands, all ye people; shout unto God with the voice of triumph." Psalm 48:1 says, "Great is the Lord, and greatly to be praised." Notice the *hands* and *voice* are used in acknowledging God's greatness. It is not a whisper; it is a shout of triumph!

Worship is not thanksgiving; it is telling Him how great He is. Worship is paying divine honors to God. It is reverencing Him, giving Him adoration and acknowledging that He is the only supreme God. Worship is a form of humility, for it acknowledges that God alone is powerful and deserves all the glory and honor.

Psalm 33:8-9 says, "Let all the earth fear the Lord: let all the inhabitants of the world stand in awe of him. For he spake, and it was done; he commanded, and it stood fast." It is important to stand in awe of the Lord and show Him great respect, for "The Lord reigneth, he is clothed with majesty" (Psalm 93:1).

In the following verses we are instructed to worship the Lord:

a. "For he is thy Lord...worship thou him" (Psalm 45:11).

b. "Give unto the Lord the glory due unto his name; worship the Lord in the beauty of holiness" (Psalm 29:2).

c. "Give unto the Lord the glory due unto his name; bring an offering, and come into his courts. O worship the Lord in the beauty of holiness: fear before him, all the earth" (Psalm 96:8-9).

d. "Thou shalt worship the Lord thy God, and him only shalt thou serve" (Matthew 4:10).

e. "Make a joyful noise unto God, all ye lands: Sing forth the honour of his name: make his praise glorious. Say unto God, How terrible art thou in thy works! through the greatness of thy power shall thine enemies submit themselves unto thee. All the earth shall worship thee, and shall sing unto thee; they shall sing to thy name" (Psalm 66:1-4).

f. "Let them exalt him also in the congregation of the people" (Psalm 107:32).

Great men and women of the Bible *worshipped* God. The known and the unknown in the Bible *worshipped* God. Those who worshipped in the Bible were blessed of God. Those who worship in this present day are blessed of God. Worshippers have a special place in God's heart.

Worshipping is a bowing down of self in the presence of Deity. It is acknowledging His great power and ability to perform miracles.

Throughout the Bible worshipping God was a very integral part of the lives of those who believed in the true God. The act of worship was demonstrated in the following examples:

Abraham's servant: "And the man bowed down his head, and worshipped the Lord. And he said, Blessed be the Lord God of my master Abraham, who hath not left destitute my master of his mercy and his truth" (Genesis 24:26-27). God had led the servant to find a bride for Isaac, and he was thankful. He showed his thankfulness by worshipping God.

Moses: "And the Lord descended in the cloud, and stood with him there...And Moses made haste, and bowed his head toward the earth and worshipped" (Exodus 34:5, 8).

Gideon: "And it was so, when Gideon heard the telling of the dream, and the interpretation thereof, that he worshipped, and returned into the host of Israel, and said, Arise: for the Lord hath delivered into your hand the host of Midian" (Judges 7:15).

David: "Then David arose from the earth, and washed, and anointed himself, and changed his apparel, and came into the house of the Lord, and worshipped" (II Samuel 12:20).

Congregation: "And David said to all the congregation, Now bless the Lord your God. And all the congregation blessed the Lord God of their fathers, and bowed down their heads, and worshipped the Lord" (I Chronicles 29:20).

Jehosphaphat: "And Jehosphaphat bowed his head with his face to the ground: and all Judah and the inhabitants of Jerusalem fell before the Lord, worshipping the Lord" (II Chronicles 20:18).

All the People: "And Ezra blessed the Lord, the great God. And all the people answered, Amen, with lifting up their hands: and they bowed their heads, and worshipped the Lord with their faces to the ground" (Nehemiah 8:8).

Job: "Then Job arose, and rent his mantle, and shaved his head, and fell down upon the ground, and worshipped" (Job 1:20).

The leper: "And behold, there came a leper and worshipped him, saying, Lord, if thou wilt, thou canst make me clean. And Jesus put forth his hand and touched him, saying, I will; be thou clean. And immediately his leprosy was cleansed" (Matthew 8:2-3).

A ruler: "While he [Jesus] spake these things unto them, behold, there came a certain ruler, and worshipped him, saying, My daughter is even now dead: but come and lay thy hand upon her, and she shall live...he went in, and took her by the hand, and the maid arose" (Matthew 9:18, 25).

They that were in the ship: "Then they that were in the ship came and worshipped him, saying, Of a truth thou art the Son of God" (Matthew 14:33).

Four and twenty elders: "And the four beasts said, Amen. And the four and twenty elders fell down and worshipped him that liveth for ever and ever" (Revelation 5:14).
"And the four and twenty elders, which sat before God on their seats, fell upon their faces, and worshipped God, Saying, We give thee thanks, O Lord God Almighty, which art, and wast, and art to come; because thou hast taken to thee thy great power, and hast reigned" (Revelation 11:16).

Although many of the Bible characters fell to the ground in humility when they worshipped God, women can worship either standing up or sitting down, if the attitude of their heart is kneeling humbly before His great presence.

Through the years I have seen women worship in a variety of ways. In my mind's eye I can see some of them.

There is sweet elder Mildred Watts, who just recently had been healed of cancer, sitting quietly with tears running down her cheeks. Then there is dear Donna Hogue worshipping with a smile on her face. Pass over to Catrina Klee, with her children seated around her. Her face is uplifted towards the heavens with a look of purity and God's glory resting upon it. Gazing around the room I see many women from different walks of life who truly love the Lord and are manifesting that love through worship in their own way. The women are not there to impress one another; they are there to lift up the Lord and draw closer to Him.

Step 3: Share the Word

Without the Word, there would be no prayer meeting; for it is the Word that expounds what prayer can do. All prayer meetings should allow time for the Word of God to be shared. Prayer is indispensable, essential and powerful, but the Word is just as vital! They must go together. One without the other is incomplete!

Women need to develop a love for the Bible. A poor blind girl who lived in France did just that. Someone gave her the Gospel of Mark in raised letters and she learned to read it by the tips of her fingers. Through constant reading, these became calloused, and her sense of touch diminished until she could not distinguish the characters. One day, she cut the skin from the ends of her fingers to increase their sensitivity, only to destroy it.

She felt like she must now give up her beloved Book, and weeping, pressed it to her lips, saying, "Farewell,

farewell, sweet Word of my Heavenly Father!" To her surprise, her lips, more delicate than her fingers, discerned the form of the letters. All night she read with her lips the Word of God and overflowed with joy at this new acquirement.

For women to gain a love for the Word such as this, it is important every time they meet for prayer that a portion of the Bible be given them. The Word is the most precious thing a woman can take with her. It will take her successfully through the fire and through the rain.

In early American history, the Pony Express ran from St. Joseph, Missouri, to Sacramento, California, a distance of 1,900 miles. The trip was made in ten days. Forty men, each riding 50 miles a day, dashed along the trail on 500 of the best horses the West could provide.

To conserve weight, clothing was very light, saddles were small and thin, and no weapons were carried. The horses themselves wore small shoes or none at all. The mail pouches were flat and very conservative in size. Yet, each rider carried a full-sized Bible! It was presented to him when he joined the Pony Express, and he took it with him despite all the weight precautions.

The Bible is the one most important thing that women need to take on their strenuous ride through life, with all its pitfalls, dangers and adverse conditions. The Bible will help them reach their destination. Not only reach it, but arrive there successfully.

The Bible gives women many incredible things too numerous to mention, but some of the wonderful things are listed here:

1. It gives women something solid to stand upon!

The Bible is without question the irrefutable Word of God—women can stake their life on it! It will not let them down.

Dr. J.O. Kinnaman said, "Of the hundreds of thousands of artifacts found by the archaeologists, not one has ever been discovered that contradicts or denies one word, phrase, clause, or sentence of the Bible, but always confirms and verifies the facts of the Biblical record." [2]

It is accurate! Over 100 years ago, William Ramsay, a young English scholar, went to Asia Minor with the expressed purpose of proving that the history given by Luke in his gospel and in the Acts was inaccurate. He began to dig in the ancient ruins of Greece and Asia Minor, testing for ancient terms, boundaries, and other items which would be a dead giveaway if a writer had been inventing this history at a later date as had been claimed by some. To his amazement, he found that the New Testament Scriptures were accurate to the tiniest detail. So convincing was the evidence that Ramsay himself became a great biblical scholar.

I have stood on the Word when there was nothing else to stand on. Facts were ominous, situations were bad, nothing looked good; in fact, everything seemed impossible as far as the natural eye could see. When everything else said *no*, the Word said *yes*, and that is what I believed! Did it work? Oh yes, it worked! God has done many great things for me. I have seen Him work miracles in many impossible situations. His Word has never failed.

Isaiah 40:8 says it like this: "The grass withereth, the flower fadeth: but the word of our God shall stand for ever."

2. It transforms and sets women free!

Horace Greeley once said, "It is impossible to mentally or socially enslave a Bible-reading people. The principles of the Bible are the groundwork of human freedom." [3]

In the true story of the *Mutiny on the Bounty*, one part that deserves retelling was the transformation wrought by the Bible. Nine mutineers with six native men and twelve native women put ashore on Pitcairn Island in 1790. One sailor soon began distilling alcohol, and the little colony was plunged into debauchery and vice.

Ten years later, only one white man survived, surrounded by native women and their children. In an old chest from the *Bounty*, this sailor one day found a Bible. He began to read it and then to teach it to the others. The result was that his own life and ultimately the lives of all those in the colony were changed. Discovered in 1808 by the *USS Topas,* Pitcairn had become a prosperous community with no jail, no whisky, no crime, and no laziness.

Women who consistently study the Bible are the happiest and most liberated women in the world. Jesus said in John 8:32, "And ye shall know the truth, and the truth shall make you free." Women's lives are definitely changed from worse to good or from good to better. The Word improves any situation, enriches any life and improves any relationship.

3. It gives women faith!

Dwight D. Eisenhower once said, "To read the Bible is to take a trip to a fair land where the spirit is strengthened and faith renewed." [4]

Prayer and faith are linked together in the book of Jude. "But ye, beloved, building up yourselves on your most holy faith, praying in the Holy Ghost" (Jude 1:20).

Not only is faith built up inside a woman through prayer, but faith is generated by the Word of God. "So then faith cometh by hearing, and hearing by the word of God" (Romans 10:17).

This happened when Paul was in Macedonia. He and Silas went out of the city to pray down by the riverside. After prayer, they sat down and spoke about the things of God to the women who were there. Acts 16:14 tells what happened: "And a certain woman named Lydia, a seller of purple, of the city of Thyatira, which worshipped God, *heard* us: whose heart the Lord opened, that she attended unto the things which were *spoken* of Paul."

When the Word is spoken, and someone hears it, there must be some kind of reaction. Faith will spring up or doubt will lift its ugly head. This is proven in the parable Jesus told about the Sower and the Seed. The four seeds that were sown fell on the following types of soil:

a. *Wayside soil*: They hear, but the devil steals the Word away from them before it takes root.

b. *Stony soil*: They hear with joy, but because they have no root system, the seed dies when trials and tribulations come.

c. *Thorny soil*: The Word that goes forth is choked with cares, riches and pleasures. The desire for the Word is not there because they allow the abundance of material things to take the place of *soul food*.

d. *Good soil*: This is the soil that is usually found in the prayer room. It depicts an honest and good heart, which loves the Word and guards against anything stealing it away. Not only does it receive the Word, but it becomes fruitful, sharing the Word with others.

4. It gives women inspiration!

Testifying before the Senate Agriculture Committee on the value of the peanut, George Washington Carver, who as an infant was traded for a broken-down race horse, said that he got his knowledge of peanuts from the Bible. Asked what the Bible said about peanuts he replied, "The Bible does not teach anything regarding the peanut. But it told me about God, and God told me about the peanut." [5]

We have had women come into the prayer room confused and depressed, but after hearing a *word* from God, the confusion and depression leaves. They come in full of anxiety, listless and afraid, but after receiving the Word, they are filled with excitement, energy and hope.

5. It gives women wisdom!

Psalm 119:104: "Through thy precepts I get understanding."

Psalm 119:130: "The entrance of thy words giveth light; it giveth understanding unto the simple."

Proverbs 4:7: "Wisdom is the principal thing; therefore get wisdom: and with all thy getting get understanding."

Proverbs 9:10: "The fear of the Lord is the beginning of wisdom: and the knowledge of the holy is understanding."

Proverbs 2:6: "For the Lord giveth wisdom: out of his mouth cometh knowledge and understanding."

II Timothy 3:15, 16: "...thou hast known the holy scriptures, which are able to make thee wise unto salvation through faith which in Christ Jesus. All scripture is given by inspiration of God..."

6. It gives women power!

George W. Truett shares the following story:

When William IV of England died, there was a young girl spending the night at the palace. They awakened her and told her that she was now the Queen of England. As soon as she heard the news she dropped on her knees and asked the Heavenly Father to help and guide her through all the years that were to follow.

For 64 years this girl, Queen Victoria, reigned over the British Empire. England never made greater progress than during her reign. A prince of India asked her what was the secret of England's power, and for her answer she quietly picked up a Book from the table nearby, "This is the secret," she said. The Book was God's Word, the Bible.

Hebrews 4:12: "For the word of God is quick, and powerful, and sharper than any twoedged sword, piercing even to the dividing asunder of soul and spirit, and of the joints and marrow, and is a discerner of the thoughts and intents of the heart."

7. It gives women light and enlightenment!

When prayer and the Word are mixed together, the result is an explosion of great light in the soul, mind and spirit. The darkness of the mind is pierced by the bright light of truth. Psalm 27:1 says, "The Lord is my light and my salvation; whom shall I fear?"

As women draw nigh to God, they come in contact with Light! Psalm 104:1-2 substantiates this: "Bless the Lord, O my soul. O Lord my God, thou art very great; thou art clothed with honour and majesty. Who coverest thyself with light as with a garment." God is covered with light! He is Light! When women make contact with the Light, they feel its effect.

Walter Knight says,

> Light is the source of all life. All vegetation would wilt and die without light. Light and joy are inseparably related. Birds greet light at dawn with joyous song. Light imparts loveliness—redness to the cherry and tints to the rose. Spiritual life, joy, and beauty come from Jesus: "I am come that they might have life" (John 10:10); "I have spoken...that my joy might remain in you, and that your joy might be full" (John 15:11). [6]

When His words penetrate the hearts of women, there is illumination and light. Psalm 119:130 says, "The entrance of thy words giveth light; it giveth understanding unto the simple."

His Word lights their pathway; it shows them the way. "Thy word is a lamp unto my feet, and a light unto my path" (Psalm 119:105).

Women can go into a prayer meeting not knowing which way to turn. They can feel tortured and confused in their thoughts, but when they come in contact with the Lord Jesus, the Light of the World (John 8:12), who was God manifested in the flesh (John 1:1-14; I Timothy 3:16), there is a transformation! A change takes place. Psalm 19:7-8 says, "The law of the Lord is perfect, converting the soul: the testimony of the Lord is sure, making wise the simple. The statutes of the Lord are right, rejoicing the heart: the commandment of the Lord is pure, enlightening the eyes." When women go into the prayer meeting, they cannot see, but when they come out, they can!

God lights their candle! Psalm 18:28 says, "For thou wilt light my candle; the Lord my God will enlighten the darkness."

The following incident, shared by a preacher, could be told over and over about those who have come into contact with the Light:

> While preaching, I noticed a nurse under deep conviction of sin. She sat night after night the picture of dejection and distress. One night she yielded herself to Christ. The burden of sin fell from her heart. She became radiant. On the way home that night she stopped at a store to do some shopping. A clerk who had known her for some time

said, "Why, you look as if someone had just lighted a candle inside you!"

"That's right," said the converted nurse.

"What I mean," said the clerk, "is that you look as if you had just fallen in love!" "I have!" exclaimed the nurse. "I have fallen in love with the One who loved me when I didn't love Him—Jesus!"

Jeremiah 23:29 says, "Is not my word like as a fire?" Fire gives light and brightens the darkness. Jesus is the Word made flesh. John 1:14 says, "And the Word was made flesh, and dwelt among us, (and we beheld his glory, the glory as of the only begotten of the Father,) full of grace and truth."

It is God's will that His children would experience light and power. He came to give abundant life (John 10:10). He came to give revelation and truth. Jesus said, "If ye continue in my word, then are ye my disciples indeed; And ye shall know the truth, and the truth shall make you free" (John 8:31-32).

God wants to give His children a revelation of who He is. When they know Him, then they will be strong. "...the people that do know their God shall be strong, and do exploits" (Daniel 11:32). Ephesians 1:17-19 says,

"That the God of our Lord Jesus Christ, the Father of glory, may give unto you the spirit of wisdom and revelation in the knowledge of him: The eyes of your understanding being enlightened; that ye may know what is the hope of his calling, and what the riches of the glory of his inheritance in the saints, And what is the exceeding greatness of his power to usward who believe, according to the working of his mighty power."

Light comes from heaven and is associated with God:

a. *Luke* 2:9:"And, lo, the angel of the Lord came upon them, and the glory of the Lord *shone* round about them: and they were sore afraid."

b. *Acts 9:3:* "And as he [Saul] journeyed, he came near Damascus; and suddenly there shined round about him, a light from heaven."

c. *Acts 12:7:* "And, behold, the angel of the Lord came upon him, and a light shined in the prison: and he smote Peter on the side, and raised him up, saying, Arise up quickly. And his chains fell off from his hands." The Lord wants the chains that have women bound, to fall off them. He wants them to be free.

d. *Ephesians 5:14:* "...Christ shall give thee light."

e. *Exodus 14:19-20:* "And the angel of God, which went before the camp of Israel, removed and went behind them; and the pillar of the cloud went from before their face, and stood behind them And it came between the camp of the Egyptians and the camp of Israel; and it was a cloud and darkness to them, but it gave light by night to these; so that the one came not near the other all night." God kept His children hidden from their enemy. He was their light in the darkness.

f. *Daniel 2:22:* "He revealeth the deep and secret things: he knoweth what is in the darkness, and the light dwelleth with him."

g. *Revelation 22:5:* "And there shall be no night there; and they need no candle, neither light of the sun; for the Lord God giveth them light."

It is when women meet together, pray together and study the Word together that God's light shines upon them and enlightenment comes.

Step 4: Prayer Needs and Praises

After the initial steps are taken—individual prayers, worship, and the sharing of the Word—the group can pray for the individual prayer needs and also share praise reports.

When women ask for prayer concerning their needs, there are various ways to respond to the requests. If the need is a physical one such as a sickness, sometimes we lay hands on them and pray for them. We have learned to speak to the sickness and tell it to go in Jesus' name!

Sometimes we join hands and pray fervently for needs that seem to be impossible. We also receive requests both in the mail and e-mail. With these, many times we lay hands on the paper, calling out the need before the throne of God.

Part II: WAYS TO PRAY

1. Worshipful Praying—Praise and Thanksgiving

The following scriptures give instructions on how to enter into the presence of the Lord and what to do when gathered together:

- *Psalm 95:2:* "Let us come before his presence with thanksgiving, and make a joyful noise unto him with psalms."
- *Psalm 100:4:* "Enter into his gates with thanksgiving, and into his courts with praise: be thankful unto him, and bless his name."
- *Psalm 34:3:* "O magnify the Lord with me, and let us exalt his name together."

The purpose of the prayer meeting is to talk to God and to exalt Him in all that is done.

Two Biblical women who exalted God and were instrumental in being a part of God's great plan were Hannah and Mary. There is a strong resemblance between the prayer of Hannah, the mother of Samuel, and the prayer of Mary, the mother of Jesus.

Mary's Song	*Hannah's Song*
My soul doth magnify the Lord	My heart rejoiceth in the Lord,
And my spirit hath rejoiced in God	Mine horn is exalted in the Lord;
He hath shewed strength with his arm;	The bows of the mighty are broken.
He hath scattered the proud in the imaginations of their hearts.	And they that stumbled are girded with strength.
He hath put down the mighty from their seats.	The Lord killeth, and maketh alive:
And exalted them of low degree.	He bringeth down to the grave and bringeth up;
He hath filled the hungry with good things;	They that were full have hired out themselves for bread;
And the rich he hath sent empty away.	And they that were hungry ceased. [7]

Both Hannah and Mary entered into God's presence by adoration, thanksgiving and great praise. Praise is the golden entrance to God's heart. Jack R. Taylor describes the "Court of Prayer" as follows:

> Praise has to do with adulations directed to God for who He is rather that what He has done. This is the court of prayer. I am convinced that this is how we get into praying in the Spirit. Praise is a facet of prayer about which the average Christian knows so very little. Yet it is vital that we learn to praise, for the vitality of every kind of prayer rests on praise. [8]

2. Praying in the Spirit

Paul instructs the Christian warrior to fight against principalities with the weapon of prayer. "Praying always with all prayer and supplication in the Spirit, and watching thereunto with all perseverance" (Ephesians 6:18).

Dr. J. H. Jowett sheds light on Ephesians 6:18 in the following excerpt from "The Illustrated Missionary News," in 1911:

> How ought this great business of prayer to be done? First replies this expert apostle, "*in the spirit*" That distinguishes true prayer from all professed prayer which takes its rise upon the doorstep of the lips. Again, it is to be done "*always*," says the expert. Prayer to him was not the exercise of an hour, but the mood of a life. And what other implication is in the great apostle's conception of prayer? "*And watching thereunto in all perseverance*." It is surely reasonable, when we have fired a projectile, to watch if it has hit the mark. It is surely reasonable, when we pray for the

illumination of China, to keep vigilant eyes perseveringly looking for the morning, and, when any consecrated scout comes home, to question him and say, "Watchman, what of the night?" 9

Dr. Jowett is saying that a true prayer is inside of us; it is a mood. It stays with us until it is answered. He says we are to be vigilant about seeking after an answer until it is done. It should be something we are interested in, not some fleeting whim. There should be a fervency, a persistence that should fill our being. We are to pray until!

There are two kinds of prayers: Those with understanding and those without. Prayers with understanding are formulated by your mind. You know exactly what you are saying. You outline the prayer, you touch every point; all the bases are covered. These prayers can be written out or spoken. They are desperate cries from the heart.

There is another kind of prayer, the kind without understanding. You do not know what you are saying, but the Spirit does. Romans 8:26 says, "Likewise the Spirit also helpeth our infirmities: for we know not what we should pray for as we ought: but the Spirit itself maketh intercession for us with groanings which cannot be uttered." How does the Spirit pray? Jude 20 says, "But ye, beloved, building up yourselves on your most holy faith, praying in the Holy Ghost."

How does one pray in the Holy Ghost? Paul said in I Corinthians 14:14, "For if I pray in an unknown tongue, my spirit prayeth, but my understanding is unfruitful." He also said, "I thank my God I speak with tongues more than ye all" (I Corinthians 14:18). Paul is telling the Corinthian church that in his *prayer* time, he prayed with other tongues; it was the Spirit praying through him. He said, "Yet in the church I had rather speak five words with my understanding, that by my voice I might teach others also, than ten thousand words in an unknown tongue" (I Corinthians 14:19).

Paul is speaking about two different settings here: The first is during his time of prayer, when he is *talking to God.* The second is when he goes to church, when he is *talking about God* so that others can know God also. When people are gathered together to learn about God, there must be words spoken that they can understand. When people are gathered together to pray to God, then at times the Spirit will make intercession in an unknown tongue. The *pray-er* does not know what she is saying, but the Spirit does. Some call it a *prayer language.*

3. Specific Praying

Charles G. Finney once said,

> A man must have some definite object before his mind. He cannot pray effectually for a variety of objects at once. The mind of man is so constituted that it cannot fasten its desires intensely upon many things at the same time. All the instances of effectual prayer recorded in the Bible were of this kind. Wherever you see that the blessing sought for in prayer was attained, you will find that the prayer which was offered was prayer for that definite object. [10]

Jesus spoke in the following passage about praying specifically, with a definite object:

> Ask, and it shall be given you; seek, and ye shall find; knock, and it shall be opened unto you: For every one that asketh receiveth; and he that seeketh findeth; and to him that knocketh it shall be opened. Or what man is there of you, whom if his son ask bread, will he give him a stone? Or if he ask a fish, will he give him a serpent? If ye then, being evil, know how to give good gifts unto your children, how much more shall your Father which is in heaven give good things to them that ask him? (Matthew 7:7-11).

The specific things asked for were bread and fish. You may say, "Well, God knows what I need; why doesn't He just send it?" Because He has established a principle in His Word. He will not violate His Word. His plan is for His children to ask Him specifically for a need. He wants them to talk to Him. He wants to be a part of their life, intricately woven together with them.

He is saying, "Talk to Me! Tell Me what it is you need." He states how to approach Him in Hebrews 4:16: "Let us therefore come boldly unto the throne of grace, that we may obtain mercy, and find grace to help in time of need."

Boldly, means "without hesitation." J.B. Rotherham in *The Emphasized New Testament: A New Translation*, translates Hebrews 4:16 this way, "Let us then be approaching with freedom of speech unto the throne of favour." To approach God boldly means to approach without restraint, to be confident and assured.

In printing, the term *bold-faced*, means "having a conspicuous or heavy face of type." It stands out more than the standard type. It gets the attention quickest from the reader's eye.

One of the definitions of *bold* is audacious. Audacious means "to be daring, spirited or adventurous." Another of its definitions is "to show contempt for the restraints of law, religion or decorum." Decorum is observance of the proprieties or conformity to accepted standards. What would happen if God's children went boldly unto God, showing contempt for the natural laws that govern their situation? What would happen if people started believing God's Word and acting according to what the Word said, instead of being conformed to how people expected them to act in the time of trouble or crisis?

When women begin to pray and touch God, they break out of the mold. They do not respond to their situation in a normal way. Instead they begin to take authority and cast down strongholds which are not rooted in God. They lose society's decorum which says, "Be cast down in your spirit, feel sorry, discouraged and depressed." God's way says, "But I will hope continually and will yet praise thee more and more" (Psalm 71:14). Women who know their God and pray specific prayers begin to dance on top of their problem, because they, like the Apostle Paul, know whom they believe. Paul expressed it this way, "For I know whom I have believed, and am persuaded that he is able to keep that which I have committed unto him against that day" (II Timothy 1:12).

The Patriarch Abraham was persuaded that God would perform what He had promised. "And being not weak in faith, he considered not his own body now dead, when he was about an hundred years old, neither yet the deadness of Sarah's womb: He staggered not at the promise of God through unbelief; but was strong in faith, giving glory to God; And being fully persuaded that, what he had promised, he was able also to perform" (Romans 4:19-21).

Women who pray are likewise persuaded that their specific prayers will be answered.

THROUGHOUT THE BIBLE, GOD ANSWERS SPECIFIC PRAYERS

- *Abraham*: "So Abraham prayed unto God: and God healed Abimelech" (Genesis 20:17).

  ABIMELECH RECEIVED HEALING BECAUSE OF SPECIFIC PRAYER

- *Jonah*:   "And Jonah prayed unto the Lord his God out of the fish's belly. I went down to the bottoms of the mountains; the earth with her bars was about me for ever: yet hast thou brought up my life from corruption, O Lord my God. When my soul fainted within me I remembered the Lord: and my prayer came in unto thee, into thine holy temple. But I will sacrifice unto thee with the voice of thanksgiving; I will pay *that* that I have vowed. Salvation is of the Lord" (Jonah 2:1, 6-7, 9).

  JONAH RECEIVED DELIVERANCE BECAUSE OF SPECIFIC PRAYER

- *Moses*:   "And when the people complained, it displeased the Lord: and the Lord heard it; and his anger was kindled; and the fire of the Lord burnt among them. And the people cried unto Moses; and when Moses prayed unto the Lord, the fire was quenched" (Numbers 11:1-2).

MOSES RECEIVED DELIVERANCE BECAUSE OF SPECIFIC PRAYER

- *Hannah*: "And she was in bitterness of soul, and prayed unto the Lord, and wept sore. And she vowed a vow, and said, O Lord of hosts, if thou wilt indeed look on the affliction of thine handmaid, and remember me, and not forget thine handmaid, but wilt give unto thine handmaid a man child, then I will give him unto the Lord all the days of his life. Wherefore it came to pass, when the time was come about after Hannah had conceived, that she bare a son, and called his name Samuel, saying, Because I have asked him of the Lord" (I Samuel 1:10-11, 20).

HANNAH RECEIVED A CHILD BECAUSE OF SPECIFIC PRAYER

- *Elijah*: "And it came to pass at the time of the offering of the evening sacrifice, that Elijah the prophet came near, and said, Lord God of Abraham, Isaac, and of Israel, let it be known this day that thou art God in Israel, and that I am thy servant, and that I have done all these things at thy word. Hear me, O Lord, hear me, that this people may know that thou art the Lord God, and that thou hast turned their heart back again. Then the fire of the Lord fell and consumed the burnt-sacrifice, and the wood, and the stones, and the dust, and licked up the water that was in the trench. And when all the people saw it, they fell on their faces: and they said, The Lord, he is the God; the Lord, he is the God" (I Kings 18:36-39).

Notice that Elijah had put out a challenge before the people to make up their minds whether they were going to serve the Lord God or the false god Baal. In the hearing of the 400 prophets of Baal and all the people, he specifically said, "...the God that answereth by fire, let him be God. And all the people answered and said, It is well spoken" (I Kings 18:24).

ELIJAH RECEIVED A SUPERNATURAL ACT BECAUSE OF SPECIFIC PRAYER

- *Hezekiah*: "In those days was Hezekiah sick unto death...Then Hezekiah turned his face toward the wall, and prayed unto the Lord. And said, Remember now, O Lord, I beseech thee, how I have walked before thee in truth and with a perfect heart, and have done that which is good in thy sight. And Hezekiah wept sore..."Then came the word of the Lord to Isaiah, saying, "Go, and say to Hezekiah, Thus saith the Lord, the God of David thy father, I have heard thy prayer, I have seen thy tears: behold, I will add unto thy days fifteen years" (Isaiah 38:1-5).

HEZEKIAH RECEIVED PHYSICAL HEALING BECAUSE OF SPECIFIC PRAYER

- *Daniel*: "Then these men assembled, and found Daniel praying and making supplication before his God...So Daniel was taken up out of the den, and no manner of hurt was found upon him, because he believed in his God" (Daniel 6:11, 23).

DANIEL WAS DELIVERED FROM THE LION'S DEN BECAUSE OF SPECIFIC PRAYER

- *Peter*: "And it came to pass in those days, that she [Dorcas] was sick, and died:...But Peter put them all forth, and kneeled down, and prayed; and turning to the body said, Tabitha, arise. And she opened her eyes" (Acts 9:37, 40).

  DORCAS RECEIVED LIFE AGAIN BECAUSE OF PETER'S SPECIFIC PRAYER AND FAITH

- *Samson*: "And Samson called unto the Lord, and said, O Lord God, remember me, I pray thee, and strengthen me, I pray thee, only this once, O God, that I may be at once avenged of the Philistines for my two eyes. And Samson took hold of the two middle pillars upon which the house stood, and on which it was borne up, of the one with his right hand, and of the other with his left. And Samson said, Let me die with the Philistines. And he bowed himself with all his might; and the house fell upon the lords, and upon all the people that were therein. So the dead which he slew at his death were more than they which he slew in his life" (Judges 16:29-30).

  SAMSON RECEIVED MERCY AND STRENGTH TO DO THE IMPOSSIBLE BECAUSE OF SPECIFIC PRAYER

- *The Early Church*: "Peter therefore was kept in prison; put prayer was made without ceasing of the church unto God for him...And behold, the angel of the Lord came upon him, and a light shined in the prison: and he smote Peter on the side, and raised him up, saying, Arise up quickly. And his chains fell off from his hands...When Peter was come to himself, he said, Now I know of a surety, that the Lord hath sent his angel, and hath delivered me out of the hand of Herod" (Acts 12:5, 7, 11).

PETER WAS DELIVERED FROM PRISON BY AN ANGEL BECAUSE OF SPECIFIC PRAYER

- *Paul*: "And it came to pass, that the father of Publius lay sick of a fever and of a bloody flux: to whom Paul entered in, and prayed, and laid his hands on him, and healed him" (Acts 28:8).

PUBLIUS' FATHER RECEIVED PHYSICAL HEALING BECAUSE OF SPECIFIC PRAYER

In order for miracles to happen and prayers to be answered, specific prayer is a must. LaJoyce Martin shares the following experience how specific prayer wrought a miracle in their daughter's life in 1985:

"Mr. Martin..." The doctors could not meet my husband's searching eyes in the consultant room at the Scott-White Hospital. They looked at the floor.

Ninety miles away, I was kneeling beside the bed in the home of my parents, with a severe back injury. When the phone rang, my husband requested that my father tell me the sad news.

Our two daughters, sixteen-year-old Angela and fourteen-year-old Bethany, had started home from church in our small Audi on the night of the sixth. Angela, a fanatic about seat belts, had buckled up before leaving the parking lot. "I'll buckle up in a minute," Bethany promised, toying with a stereo cassette in the back seat. She never got the seat belt fastened.

On the well-lighted four-lane boulevard less than a mile from our home, Angela failed to turn on her headlights. A car rolled up beside her and blinked. She looked down to engage the lights on the downhill slope, and when she raised her eyes, she was dangerously close to the rear of the automobile ahead. Swerving to change lanes, she felt the car careen. Overcorrecting, she jerked the wheel the opposite direction, throwing the car into a fatal skid, and slid off the road into a large tree. Occupants of a passing vehicle heard the girls screaming and praying as the Audi jumped the curb sideways, flipped onto two wheels and bashed against the immovable object broadside. The tree lacked six inches plunging half way through the small car. The frame on the driver's side broke and the vehicle wrapped itself U-shaped about the tree, shattering glass in all directions.

My husband waited in agonizing uncertainty at the hospital. Angela would be all right he learned, but he was not allowed to see Bethany. At last the doctors came. "She's in a coma and hemorrhaging on both sides of her brain," they reported. "The brain itself is severely bruised. You can expect at least six months hospitalization. We are uncertain as to the extent of brain damage, and we are not sure we can save her right eye." In extreme critical condition, Bethany was sent to the Intensive Care Unit. Nine machines—and God—kept her alive.

One of the hardest things I had ever faced in my life was not being able to see my injured child, to hold her inert hand, to talk to her unheeding little body...and the knowledge that if she died, I would not even be able to attend her funeral. My severe back injury had made me bedfast, and I suffered fifty-six days of tortuous pain. I could not sit, stand or lie down without pain. The only relief I found was in a kneeling position.

For most of the night when we heard the news I prayed, not knowing how or what to pray, feeling a human helplessness I had never before experienced.

Around 4:00 a.m., something welled up inside of me...I called my husband at the hospital. "Honey," I said with feeling, "We need a miracle! Our church needs a miracle! Our city needs a miracle! God hasn't told us He's ready to take our Bethany, and until He does, it is our privilege to believe that He will give us one!"

The crisis came the following night. The doctor called my husband into the family counseling room. "Her brain is deteriorating," he said. "The blood vessels are giving way....Our only hope will be brain surgery if the seepage cannot be stopped. And we may lose her...." The doctor said that his wife was home praying for our daughter along with himself. "And I want to tell you how to pray *specifically*. Pray that the blood vessels in the brain stabilize."

Some fifty people joined the prayer. Special friends and neighbors, some who were not acquainted with prayer, knelt and asked God for the miracle. In one hour the report came that the process of deterioration had reversed itself. The leaking had stopped just short of the fatal loss of red blood cells.

My husband never left Bethany's side except to change clothes. Calls began to pour in from all over Texas and seventeen other states. Concerned people were praying everywhere. Doctors, nurses, neighbors, and people he did not know came with words of encouragement.

When the coma persisted into the second week, my husband's heart grew heavier and heavier. He moved to Bethany's side and spoke gently in her ear, "Bethany, we're going to pray." As he asked God to bring her out of the coma, Bethany's lips began to move and she opened her eyes. She was praying, too.

On July 26, 1985, twenty days after her accident, Bethany walked out of the hospital with her carload of stuffed animals, sucker bouquets, and balloons. She went to church that night. The insurance adjuster came to view the totally demolished car. "Angela's seat belt saved her," she said, "but had Bethany had her seat belt fastened, the impact would have killed her instantly." God thinks of even the little details. [11]

Author's Note: In this chapter we gave Sharing the Word as one of the steps in conducting the Prayer Meeting. To help you with this, I have written a study book to go with this book. It is eighty pages filled with 52 short lessons. There is a lesson for each week of the year, and is broken down according to month and subject. It is entitled *At the Master's Feet, Volume I.*

Prayer is as vast as God because He is behind it. Prayer is as mighty as God, because He has committed Himself to answer it."

Leonard Ravenhill [1]

5
For Women Learning to Pray

This chapter will give instructions for those who do not know how to pray. Chapter 4 gave the ideal way to begin a women's prayer meeting. However, if you do not have a place to meet, if you have no leader, if you are not skilled in the Word, even if you do not know how to pray, do not let that stop you. If you desire to pray for your children, your home, or your needs with other women, then do so. Remember: a prayer meeting can begin with *you*!

A. PRAYER BY SUBJECT

To help you get started, begin to pray by talking to the Lord by subject. You can pray the following prayers together or you can have one woman pray the prayer for all of you. Close your eyes and begin to call on the Lord from the depths of your soul. Paul gave some instructions on how to pray in Colossians 3:17: "And whatsoever ye do in word or deed, do all in the name of the Lord Jesus, giving thanks to God and the Father by him." So learn to pray in the name of Jesus, that name above every name.

1. Pray for your children—for protection, help in life, wisdom, salvation, and if need be, deliverance from drugs, alcoholism, lust, rebellion and any other things that have them bound.

Dear Jesus, Set my children free from the bondages of sin. Deliver them from the things that have them bound. (List whatever it is they are struggling with: drugs, lust, rebellion, etc.) May they know the power of the resurrection in their life. Give them hope and confidence in You.

I pray that my children will receive and love you as their Savior. Help them to understand that You loved them and gave Your life for them, that You came so that they might be set free from the bondages of sin and have abundant life.

Let them commit their lives to You. Fill them with Your Holy Spirit. Let them be transformed by the renewing of their mind (Romans 12:2). Help them to trust in You and be not afraid in these days that are filled with such violence. Help them to seek You and Your understanding. Put a hunger in their heart to know You. Deliver them from the snare of the enemy.

Let the peace of God dwell in their hearts. Give them confidence to face the pressures of life. Let them know that You are with them and that You will guide them

118

each step of the way if they will learn to listen to Your voice.

Protect my children, cover them with Your blood, put a hedge around them. We bind the power of the enemy that would hurt them. Keep them from evil. Deliver them from that which would harm them.

Let my children love the Word of God. Let them base their standard of living on Your Word and not on society's voice, for Your Word is a light that penetrates all darkness. Write Your Word on their hearts so that they will be obedient to truth and to the way of true freedom. Let them know the higher road of living. Help them to become fulfilled, happy and successful in God.

Guide my children in all that they do. Let them build their lives on truth, wisdom and love. Help my children to understand that You want to dwell inside of them and that their body is the temple for the Holy Spirit to dwell in. Let them be reminded of Your love when they would be tempted to defile themselves.

Help my children to develop healthy friendships. Give them friends who are true, wholesome and who believe in You.

Keep their minds pure. Let them be transformed by the renewing of their mind through the power of the Word and of Your Spirit. Give them victory over evil thoughts, and may they think on things which are true, noble, right, pure, lovely, excellent and worthy of praise (Phillippians. 4:8).

Help my children to become what You created them to be. Help them find their life's work and their life's partner. Keep them happily engaged in a worthy cause and happily married throughout life. Let them walk together in love, understanding and unity.

Lord, help develop the fruit of Your spirit in them: love, joy, peace, patience, kindness, goodness, faithfulness, gentleness and self-control. May our children bring glory to you and honor to their families.

When they would walk through trials and difficulties, help them to keep an optimistic, faithful attitude. Let them not become scarred and negative, but let them learn that all things work together for good if they will lean upon You. Teach them Your way and let them become better instead of bitter.

When my children are hurting, Lord, be their comfort. Let Your grace and mercy be extended unto them. May they know that the secret hiding place in the midst of the storm is in the shadow of the Almighty.

Help me to be a good and wise mother today and show my children how to find You. May Your face shine upon our family and grant unto us this day peace, blessing and understanding. Let us stand strong in the midst of the storm and learn to be overcomers in spite of what faces us. We give you all praise, honor and glory, and believe that You are working in our behalf, for which we will always be thankful to You!

In Jesus' Name, Amen

2. Pray for your husband.

Jesus, we ask You today to work in the lives of our husbands. Help each husband to know that You love him and that You want to help him as he works hard to help provide for his family.

Help him to walk according to Your plan and to follow Your way. Guide his footsteps and let him learn of You. Help him to talk to You and share his frustrations with You.

Keep his mind pure and let him learn to meditate on the Word of God, so that he may be successful and happy. Help him to hate sin and flee from evil!

Let him walk godly before You, being an example for those who are following after him. Help him to feel fulfilled while he works on the job. Give him answers when hard things press up against him. Show him the way when their seems to be no way.

Let other men who are trustworthy and loyal be his friends. Let them be friends who will influence him for good and not be a drain on him spiritually. Let him associate with men of character who will build him up and not tear him down.

Give him confidence in his daily walk, confidence on the job and confidence in You. Let him know that You are on his side and that no weapon formed against him can prosper—You will fight for him and he will win.

Give him wisdom today. Let my husband walk according to your Word and not lean unto his own understanding.

Help my husband to love as You taught about love in I Corinthians 13. Let us love one another and learn to forgive one another when we would grow angry with each other. Help him to forgive and let our marriage be strengthened.

Give my husband the gift of faith. Let him believe in God even when the situation makes it appear that all is lost. Help him to stand firm on Your Word and believe for a miracle!

Give him peace when the storms of life rage! Wrap Your arms around him and let him know that You will never leave or forsake him. Let him not be afraid, but let him trust in the Lord.

Strengthen his body and let him walk in health. Put a song in his heart so that he can rejoice even when things are bad. Let him rejoice in You and Your promises.

Let him know truth for the truth shall set him free. Let him be filled with Your Holy Spirit. Let him walk in holiness and temperance and grant him self-control. Set his thoughts on things above. Do not let him sink to things that would destroy him.

May he know You in the power of your resurrection and walk in accordance with Your Word. Give him help to overcome every temptation. Keep him free from the influence of Satan and help him to resist him when he would try to make him fall.

In Jesus' Name, Amen

3. Pray for physical healing.

Dear Jesus,

We are told in Isaiah 53:5 that You were wounded for our transgressions, You were bruised for our iniquities, and with Your stripes we are healed. Lord, let that healing power flow through my body today.

Eradicate all sickness and disease. Cleanse me from all infection and that which should not be. Let the blood of Jesus be applied to the infected area, and may it be washed clean by the blood of the Lamb.

I Peter 2:24 says that by Your stripes we were healed. The work was already done at Calvary, Lord, and I accept Your healing today.

Lord, grant me faith to believe Your Word for my healing, for You said, "If thou canst believe all things are possible to him that believeth" (Mark 9:23).

It is Your will for me to be healed, for You said in III John 2, "Beloved, I wish above all things that thou mayest prosper and be in health, even as thy soul prospereth." Lord, wash my soul and make me clean so that I do not harbor sickly thoughts. Let the power of Your Word cleanse me and cut out all strongholds of disease. Let me walk in newness of life.

You promised that I could have my prayers answered if they were the will of God. III John says that it is your will for me to be in health. I John 5:14-15 says, "And this is the confidence that we have in him, that, if we ask any thing according to his will, he heareth us. And if we know that he hear us, whatsoever we ask, we know that we have the petitions that we desired of him."

Thank You for hearing my prayer; thank You for healing me. Thank You for directing me into the proper lifestyle that encourages healthful living. Let me learn how to work with God's laws and not against them.

I speak to the mountain of sickness and command it to leave and be cast into the sea as you stated to do in Mark 11:23. I know that You are doing a work in my body right now.

As You healed the lame man by the gate Beautiful in Acts 3, it was the power *of* Your name and the faith *in* Your name that caused the healing to take place. Your name is above every name. All power in heaven and earth is subject to that name. I rise out of this bed in the name of Jesus, knowing that it is a name that is highly exalted and all sickness and disease is subject to that name. I bind all the forces of sickness and the spirit of fear and cast them out in Jesus' name!

Give me a song in my heart. Make me joyful, for a merry heart does good like a medicine. Let me sing, laugh and rejoice in the God of my salvation and healing.

Help me to hide the Word of God in my heart, for it is life to me. As You sent Your Word and healed them in the New Testament, so let Your Word heal me today and give me a new lease on life.

I bind the forces of hell that would try to deplete and destroy me, and cast them out. I loose healing power, faith and confidence in God inside of me.

I give You all honor and glory and thank You for the love of God that is made alive in my heart. I thank You that You are strengthening me by Your Spirit.

All praise be to God who is able to do exceeding abundantly above all we ask or think. Be glorified in me today by healing my body so that all may know that the Lord He is God!

In Your Name, Amen

4.   Pray for financial blessing.

Dear Lord,

We come to You acknowledging that You are the source of all power. It is You who gives power to get wealth as stated in Deuteronomy 8:18. We are asking for help with our finances. We need money to pay our bills, but more than that, we need wisdom and understanding on how to be good stewards of that which You have given to us.

Teach us this day how to profit, for You said in Isaiah 48:17, "I am the Lord thy God which teacheth thee to profit, which leadeth thee by the way that thou shouldest go."

Teach us how to honor the Lord with all our substance, so that we shall have plenty as spoken in Proverbs 3:9-10.

You have promised in Psalm 32 to instruct and teach us in the way we should go, and to guide us with Your eye. Please show us the way, so that we might follow the right path of blessing, so we might bless Your kingdom and help others.

Make Your face to shine upon us; save us from financial distress. Let the blessing of the Lord make us rich today for Your glory!

Give us this day our daily bread and daily needs. Rebuke the devourer away from our home and family.

Lord, we reverence You today. Send Your Word and bless us according to Psalm 115:13-14, for it says: "He will bless them that fear the Lord, both small and great. The Lord shall increase you more and more, you and your children."

David said it well in Psalm 37:25: "I have been young, and now am old: yet have I not seen the righteous forsaken, nor his seed begging bread."

We commit our finances to You today and ask that all our needs would be met, and that we would be blessed financially, so that we can bless Your kingdom.

In Jesus' name, Amen

B. SHARE THE WORD

After prayer, it is time to study the Word. I have prepared a handbook that can be used for this purpose. It contains 52 short Bible studies—a year's supply for women's weekly prayer groups. It is entitled *At the Master's Feet.*

It is important to take time to study the Bible for it is the rock of truth. President Woodrow Wilson, 28th president of the United States, once said, "I ask every man and woman in this audience that from this day on they will realize that part of the destiny of America lies in their daily perusal of this great Book." [2]

Prayer is absolutely necessary for great things to happen, but the Word is what gives the faith and understanding for those things. These two weapons are an unbeatable combination against the enemy and will bring great victory!

After the Bible study, you can sing together and worship together. The main thing is that you touch God, share your heart with Him, and leave uplifted in your spirit. A good pattern to base your prayer meeting on is found in Colossians 3:16: "Let the word of Christ dwell in you richly in all wisdom; teaching and admonishing one another in psalms and hymns and spiritual songs, singing with grace in your hearts to the Lord."

"Our God has
boundless resources.
The only limit is in us.
Our asking, our thinking,
our praying are too small.
Our expectations are too
limited."

A. B. Simpson [1]

6
Goals for the Prayer Meeting

Anything worth doing should have purpose. A successful prayer meeting takes more that just wishing or dreaming. It costs something, but it is worth it.

> There's no free gate to anything worthwhile—not to skill nor health, nor to success nor friendship, nor even to the lasting and respect of those who are nearest and dearest to us. These are the items that make up the best income that any human being can have, and the sum of that income will be measured by the sum of what we are willing to pay to get it. 2

What should be the main goals for the prayer meeting?

GOAL NUMBER ONE: FOR CHRIST AS LORD TO HAVE THE PRE-EMINENCE

Amy Carmichael, missionary to Japan in 1892, stated the following in her 1915 diary:

> If you hold fast to the resolve that in all things Christ as Lord shall have the pre-eminence, if you keep His will, His glory, and His pleasure high above everything, and if you continue in His love, loving one another as He has loved you, then all will be well, eternally well. [3]

This resolve should be the number one goal of the prayer meeting. The time of prayer should be a gathering together of women acknowledging that Christ is Lord, that He is able to do exceeding, abundantly above anything they ask of Him. He should be seen as the one who receives the glory and honor, which places Him in an exalted position above all others.

Isaiah 6:1-5 describes what happened when Isaiah saw the Lord:

> In the year that king Uzziah died I saw also the Lord sitting upon a throne, high and lifted up, and his train filled the temple. Above it stood the seraphims: each one had six wings; with twain he covered his face, and with twain he covered his feet, and with twain he did fly. And one cried unto another, and said, Holy, holy, holy, is the Lord of hosts: the whole earth is full of his glory. And the posts of the door moved at the voice of him that cried, and the house was filled with smoke.

Then said I, Woe is me! for I am undone; because I am a man of unclean lips, and I dwell in the midst of a people of unclean lips; for mine eyes have seen the King, the Lord of hosts.

The goal of the prayer meeting is that every woman would see the Lord high and lifted up, that she would sense His glory and reverence Him as Lord. The following verses depict Him as the *most high:*

- *Psalm 7:17:* "I will praise the Lord according to his righteousness: and will sing praise to the name of the Lord *most high.*"
- *Psalm 9:2:* "I will be glad and rejoice in thee: I will sing praise to thy name, O thou *most High.*"
- *Psalm 92:1:* "It is a good thing to give thanks unto the Lord, and to sing praises unto thy name, O *most High.*"
- *Psalm 50:14:* "Offer unto God thanksgiving; and pay thy vows unto the *most High.*"
- *Psalm 57:2:* "I will cry unto God *most high*; unto God that performeth all things for me."
- *Psalm 91:1:* "He that dwelleth in the secret place of the *most High* shall abide under the shadow of the Almighty."
- *Psalm 92:8:* "But thou, Lord, art *most high* for evermore."

God is higher than the problems. He is higher than the enemy. He is higher than any circumstance that would seek to destroy you. The psalmist David recognized God as being higher than his difficulties and sang the following song: "From the end of the earth will I cry unto thee, when my heart is overwhelmed: lead me to the rock that is higher than I. For thou hast been a shelter for me, and a strong tower from the enemy" (Psalm 61:1-2).

GOAL NUMBER TWO: TO PRAY TOGETHER AS ONE

Marjorie Holmes wrote the following prayer of praise which extols the joy of praying together:

The Lord has led me into the radiant company of his people. Praise the Lord.

The Lord has given me the fellowship of others on the selfsame journey to find him.

He has given me a spiritual family. He has given me sisters in the dearest sense of the word.

To pray and worship the Lord with others who earnestly, honestly seek him, is to add new dimensions of strength and joy.

Praise the Lord for this gift of fellowship and friendship. For the miracles of work and happiness and healing that burst like stars and change the course of lives when people come together who truly love the Lord. [4]

There is not only joy, but there is also power when people unite together praying for a common cause. Dr. J. Wilbur Chapman in his first pastorate in Philadelphia was visited by a layman who frankly said to him: "You are not a strong preacher. In the usual order of things you will fail here, but a little group of laymen have agreed to gather every Sunday morning and pray for you." Dr. Chapman added: "I saw that group grow to one thousand men

134

gathered weekly to pray for this preacher." 5 Of course, he had great success.

Would to God that women would gather together and pray as one for the leaders of their church, their pastor and their homes—to pray relentlessly, fearlessly and powerfully together for one common goal!

Many women praying together are a force to be reckoned with! One woman is strong, but many women becoming one in the Spirit, are powerful! They are like the pennies in the following story:

In Jessup, Maryland, a truck carrying 4.3 million pennies turned over on an entrance ramp to a highway, dumping copper-filled canvas sacks all over the highway. Traffic was tied up for several hours while police cleared the road. One penny alone, of course, would not have held up anything, but when 4.3 million pennies were brought together, they stopped traffic. 6

It is time to stop the traffic of sin, violence, crime, divorce and the break-up of the family. It is time to join together in prayer and build a mighty memorial of prayer that will get God's attention, as was done in the case of Cornelius.

"There was a certain man in Caesarea called Cornelius, a centurion of the band called the Italian band. A devout man, and one that feared God with all his house, which gave much alms to the people, and prayed to God alway. He saw in a vision evidently about the ninth hour of the day an angel of God coming in to him, and saying unto him, Cornelius. And when he looked on him, he was afraid, and said, What is it Lord? And he said unto him, Thy prayers and thine alms are come up for a memorial before God" (Acts 10:1-4).

Prayers are forever! They never die; they are strong and powerful. How much more powerful are they when women unite together as one in prayer. They are a force to be reckoned with. Even hell trembles when women get together to pray—not to gossip, shop, work or play—but to pray.

GOAL NUMBER THREE: TO PRAY EFFECTUAL FERVENT PRAYERS

"The effectual fervent prayer of a righteous man availeth much. Elias was a man subject to like passions as we are, and he prayed earnestly that it might not rain: and it rained not on the earth by the space of three years and six months. And he prayed again, and the heaven gave rain, and the earth brought forth her fruit" (James 5:16-18).

The Bible was written for men, women and children of all nationalities and cultures. Theologians will tell you that when the Bible says *man*, it is referring to all of mankind, unless otherwise noted. For example, when Jesus was tempted by the devil, He said, "Man shall not live by bread alone" (Matthew 4:4). *Man* refers to all human beings. In the above scripture, James is showing the power of effectual fervent prayer prayed by anyone who is righteous.

When Jesus was teaching His followers to pray and not to faint, He told them a parable about a judge who did not fear God. There was a woman in the same city who went to him for help, but he would not help her. Finally, he did help her because of her consistent, fervent plea for help. "Though I fear not God, nor regard man; Yet because this widow troubleth me, I will avenge her, lest by her continual coming she weary me" (Luke 18:4-5).

Jesus further stated, "And the Lord said, Hear what the unjust judge saith. And shall not God avenge his own elect, which cry day and night unto him, though he bear long with them? And I tell you that he will avenge them speedily" (Luke 18:6-8).

The goal of the prayer meeting is to pray prayers that get answered no matter how long it takes. The women must bind together and *knock* on heaven's door until God answers their prayer!

GOAL NUMBER FOUR: TO INVOKE THE BLESSING OF THE LORD

The Lord wants His children to be blessed. He wants them to be a blessing to others and to receive a blessing. I Peter 3:9 states that they should inherit a blessing: "Not rendering evil for evil, or railing for railing: but contrariwise blessing; knowing that ye are thereunto called, that ye should inherit a blessing."

The Bible records that many were blessed of the Lord. It was God's desire that His children would be blessed. The Lord spoke to Moses and told him to bless the people in Numbers 6:24-27: "The Lord bless thee, and keep thee:

The Lord make his face shine upon thee, and be gracious unto thee: The Lord lift up his countenance upon thee, and give thee peace. And they shall put my name upon the children of Israel; and I will bless them."

God wants to give blessing. "The blessing of the Lord, it maketh rich, and he addeth no sorrow with it" (Proverbs 10:22). Psalm 3:8 says, "...thy blessing is upon thy people." A few of those specifically mentioned in the Bible as the Lord being with them or receiving a blessing are as follows:

- Abraham (Genesis 12:2).
- Joseph (Genesis 39:23).
- Joshua (Joshua 6:27).
- Daniel (Daniel 5:11; 6:27-28).
- Mary (Luke 1:28).

It is an established fact that God wants to bless His children. The following list will show how God pronounces a blessing upon a certain *kind* of people:

1. Those that trust in the Lord
Psalm 2:11-12: "Serve the Lord with fear, and rejoice with trembling...Blessed are all they that put their trust in him."

Psalm 34:8: "O taste and see that the Lord is good: blessed is the man that trusteth in him."

Psalm 40:4: "Blessed is that man that maketh the Lord his trust."

2. Those that dwell in God's house or with Him
Psalm 84:4: "Blessed are they that dwell in thy house: they will be still praising thee."

Psalm 91:1: "He that dwelleth in the secret place of the most High shall abide under the shadow of the Almighty." What a place of blessing—right next to the most high.

3. Those that fear the Lord, keep God's Word and seek Him

Psalm 119:2: "Blessed are they that keep his testimonies, and that seek him with the whole heart."

Psalm 112:1: "Blessed is the man that feareth the Lord, that delighteth greatly in his commandments."

4. Those who considereth the poor

Psalm 41:1-2: "Blessed is he that considereth the poor: the Lord will deliver him in time of trouble."

5. Those that give

Malachi 3:10: "Bring ye all the tithes into the storehouse, that there may be meat in mine house, and prove me now herewith, saith the Lord of hosts, if I will not open you the windows of heaven, and pour you out a blessing, that there shall not be room enough to receive it."

6. On the just

Proverbs 10:6: "Blessings are upon the head of the just."

7. On the faithful

Proverrbs 28:20: "A faithful man shall abound with blessings."

8. The pure in heart

Psalm 24:4-5: "He that hath clean hands, and a pure heart; who hath not lifted up his soul unto vanity, nor sworn deceitfully. He shall receive the blessing from the Lord."

Matthew 5:8: "Blessed are the pure in heart: for they shall see God."

There is a story in the Old Testament about a man whose mother named him Jabez, which meant "Because I bare him with sorrow" (I Chronicles 4:9). Rev. Sam Emory, an evangelist, once preached at Christian Life Center about Jabez and his four-point prayer. Emory said, "He had a name and a situation he could not change. He was destined for sorrow, but he prayed to God to change what he could not change, and God answered his prayer."

The Bible records the prayer of Jabez: "And Jabez called on the God of Israel, saying, Oh that thou wouldest bless me indeed, and enlarge my coast, and that thine hand might be with me, and that thou wouldest keep me from evil, that it may not grieve me! And God granted him that which he requested" (I Chronicles 4:10).

Notice that Jabez asked for a blessing. He did not just pray a blessing, but asked for a blessing *indeed*. Not only did he ask for a blessing, but he asked that God would *keep* him from evil. God did all that he prayed for! His four-point prayer was as follows:

1. Bless me Lord indeed!
2. Enlarge my coast.
3. Let your hand be with me, not against me.
4. Keep me from evil, so that I might not suffer the grief that is planned for me by the enemy.

We as women are filled with sorrow about our families, the plight of the nation, the terror and violence that fills the earth. We may not be able to change things, but if we pray to God, He can change things, just as He did for Jabez.

It should be one of the goals of the prayer meetings to pray a blessing upon each woman and the family or organization she represents.

GOAL NUMBER FIVE: TO STAND IN CHRIST'S STEAD

If Christ is the Way, we are the signboards.
If Christ is the Truth, we are the examples.
If Christ is the Life, we are the messengers.
If Christ is the Door, we are the doorkeepers, to open it to others.
If Christ is the Vine, we are the fruit bearing branches. [7]

When Jesus ascended into the heavens after his resurrection, He told His followers to wait at Jerusalem until they be endued with power from on high. After ten days of praying and waiting in an upper room, there came a sound from heaven as a rushing mighty wind, and everyone in the room was filled with the Holy Spirit.

While Jesus walked on the earth and did great miracles among the people, He kept telling His disciples and followers that they would do greater works than He had done. "Verily, verily, I say unto you, He that believeth on me, the works that I do shall he do also; and greater works than these shall he do; because I go unto my Father" (John 14:12).

Jesus stated His purpose in Luke 4:18: "The Spirit of the Lord is upon me, because he hath anointed me to preach the gospel to the poor; he hath sent me to heal the brokenhearted, to preach deliverance to the captives, and recovering of sight to the blind, to set at liberty them that are bruised."

Accordingly, these should be the aim of the prayer meeting:

1. To help heal the brokenhearted.
2. To help those who are poor and not rich in God.
3. To help set the captive free.
4. To help open the eyes of the spiritually blind.
5. To help liberate and heal the bruised.

In short, the prayer meeting becomes a spiritual hospital that ministers to those who are hurting. It should give hope to the hopeless, spread the power of the Gospel of Jesus Christ, and be a channel that the Holy Spirit can both pray and flow through.

"An hour in prayer can give the believer enough power from God to overcome the second most powerful force in the universe."

The Bible Friend [1]

7
Entering Into Spiritual Warfare

Women have an intuition about things that cannot always be visibly seen or factually known. They are sensitive to their feelings and emotions, and have often been made aware of things happening in other places of the world. Sometimes a warning, a heaviness, an insight or a prodding by the Holy Spirit comes to a woman to pray about an activity elsewhere. God even uses dreams or visions to cause a woman to pray, which have led to amazing results.

J.O. Sanders shared how this happened to his wife. He relates the following:

In 1947, while I was traveling on horseback in Central China with Mr. Fred Mitchell, we came to a spot that was notorious as a robber hide-out. The missionary accompanying us was keeping a sharp missionary accompanying us was keeping a sharp look-out.

Suddenly we came upon a body lying beside the path. The victim was obviously not long dead. The brigands had been at work.

A few days later I received a letter from my wife, asking whether we had been in any danger on a date and at a time she named. On that particular night she had been suddenly awakened with the strong impression that I was in danger. She rose and prayed until the burden lifted and peace returned. On consulting my diary, I discovered that this midnight prayer synchronized with the time we were passing through that robber-infested area. God heard and answered the prayer for the safety of His servants. 2

Think about this power! A man is in China, a woman is in America. She is awakened with a strong impression that her husband is in danger in China. She begins to pray and enter into spiritual warfare. God is directing the whole operation. He awakens her, He impresses her, and He is watching her as she crawls out of bed and begins to pray. The unseen world is at work. The evil that was meant for her husband is thwarted by this woman's prayer.

She had the power to influence what was happening in China! The most unused power in the world is the power of prayer. It is more powerful than atomic power, and is able to work miracles and cause unexplainable things to happen. In the following poem, Sandra Goodwin captures the power that is given to a woman who prays:

"Traveling On My Knees"

Last night I took a journey to a land across the seas;
I did not go by boat or plane, I traveled on my knees.
I saw so many people there in deepest depths of sin,
But Jesus told me I should go, that there were souls to win.
But I said, "Jesus, I cannot go and work with such as these."
He answered quickly, "Yes, you can by traveling on your knees."
He said, "You pray; I'll meet the need, you call and I will hear;
Be concerned about lost souls, of those both far and near."
And so I tried it, knelt in prayer, gave up some hours of ease;
I felt the Lord right by my side while traveling on my knees.
As I prayed on and saw souls saved and twisted bodies healed,
And saw God's workers' strength renewed while laboring on the field.
I said, "Yes, Lord, I have a job. My desire Thy will to please;
I can go and heed Thy call by traveling on my knees." [3]

If one woman whose husband was in China could counteract the activities of hell by praying alone, what could happen if several women would bind together in prayer? Matthew 18:19 emphatically says, "Again I say unto you, That if two of you shall agree on earth as touching any thing that they shall ask, it shall be done for them of my Father which is in heaven."

Women have the power to change negative situations both in their homes and communities. If they would bind together in prayer and begin to oppose and obstruct Satan's business, hell would be defeated and frustrated in its efforts.

In the above story, the woman was praying a *preventive prayer*. We need more preventive prayers! In our earlier example, Jabez, prayed a preventive prayer. "Oh that thou wouldest bless me indeed. . .keep me from evil, that it may not grieve me!" (I Chronicles 4:10).

Did God answer? The verse concludes with, "And God granted him that which he requested."

Spiritual warfare should include praying preventive prayers. When Jesus taught His disciples to pray, He included one in the example prayer: "Lead us not into temptation, but deliver us from evil: For thine is the kingdom, and the power, and the glory, for ever" (Matthew 6:13).

How much evil could be thwarted if women prayed more preventive prayers?

There is an unseen world that surrounds us every day. It is described in Ephesians 6:12: "For we wrestle not against flesh and blood, but against principalities, against powers, against the rulers of the darkness of this world, against spiritual wickedness in high places."

IT IS AN ESTABLISHED FACT THAT WE ARE IN SPIRITUAL WARFARE

1. We war against principalities.
2. We war against powers.
3. We war against the rulers of the darkness of this world.
4. We war against spiritual wickedness in high places.

But our weapons are mighty! "For the weapons of our warfare are not carnal, but mighty through God to the pulling down of strongholds" (II Corinthians 10:4).

In the Great War in France a strong position had to be taken. The enemy's lines were so defended by trenches, parapets and barbed wire, that any assault, however determined, by whatever number of men, must have failed. However brave the attackers might have been, not a man would have reached the enemy's trenches alive. It was, in fact, quite impossible for the place to be taken by infantry assault. But the attacking general had collected large numbers of the most powerful artillery, firing the most powerfully explosive shells. With this excessive strength of massed artillery a continuous fire was kept up for over five hours on the one objective till trenches were blown in, palisades thrown down, and wire entanglement blown to pieces.

Then, when the artillery had done its work, the waiting troops were at last able to go up "every man straight before him," and, with comparatively little loss, to capture the position. What had been absolutely impossible to them before had been possible by the sustained fire of the artillery.

I believe this is a most accurate and instructive picture of spiritual warfare. There are positions of the adversary that cannot be stormed or starved. There are defences that are impregnable. There are obstructions which effectually bar the progress of the most devoted members of God's great missionary army. Before such can possibly succeed there is necessary the sustained and continuous fire of the artillery of prayer. Nothing else will take its place. Nothing will avail until it has done its work.

Too often, in the absence of prevailing prayer, the assault has to be made without, and precious lives are sacrificed, time is lost, and all efforts are in vain; not because God is unfaithful, or the servant is not devoted, but because the artillery of prayer has been lacking, and no breach has been made in the enemy's defenses.—Northcote Deck 4

Sometimes women underestimate the power of the artillery of prayer. Continuous, unrelenting prayer petitioned with faith can tear down any stronghold of the enemy. It can bombard its strongest opponent in the unseen world of evil.

The leader of the unseen world of evil is the prince of the earth. Paul gives him recognition in Ephesians 2:2: "Wherein in times past ye walked according to the course of this world, according to the prince of the power of the air, the spirit that now worketh in the children of disobedience."

Satan is the prince of the power of the earth and the air that surrounds it. He was cast out of heaven. "How art thou fallen from heaven, O Lucifer, son of the morning! how art thou cut down to the ground" (Isaiah 14:12).

Job 1:6-7 gives insight as to the perimeters of Satan's kingdom: "Now there was a day when the sons of God came to present themselves before the Lord, and Satan came also among them. And the Lord said unto Satan, Whence comest thou? Then Satan answered the Lord and said, From going to and fro in the earth, and from walking up and down in it."

Satan is still walking to and fro in the earth, seeking whom he may devour, kill or destroy, but praying women can put him to flight and stop his advances. Darlene Malcolm, one of our prayer leaders in Stockton, wrote what happened in her life during times of prayer.

During our times of prolonged praying, God moved so powerfully. We had physical and emotional healings take place, as well as deliverances. We began to teach spiritual warfare and study the Bible, and the Lord strengthened us and encouraged us to fight until we won. He also led us by the Spirit to pray for things that were unknown to us, but He revealed them. We were able to do warfare for His causes and purposes and pray a blessing. We yielded ourselves to Him and He used us to bless many people.

Women have the power to war against Satan and win! They can speak to him and to the things which he puts on them, and tell them to go in Jesus' name. In the Shepherds Circle of Prayer, we have spoken to cancers, tumors, pain, sickness and disease and commanded them to go, dissolve or disappear. We have spoken to spirits of anxiety, fear, and depression and commanded them to go. It does not matter what you are dealing with, the power is not of man, but the power is of God; therefore, anything spoken to must go according to the Word of God.

Jesus said to speak! Speak to those mountains of sickness, doubt, fear, problems—or whatever it is that you need an answer for. Mark 11:23 says, "For verily I say unto you, That whosoever [put your name here; you are a whosoever] shall *say* unto this mountain, Be thou removed, and be thou cast into the sea; and shall not doubt in his heart, but shall believe that those things which he *saith* shall come to pass; he shall have whatsoever he *saith*."

I Peter 3:9 says to resist the devil. James 4:7 says, "Resist the devil and he will flee from you." You resist through speaking to him, and saying, as Jesus said, "It is written!" The devil finally disappeared after being attacked three times with the Word of God. "Then the devil leaveth him, and, behold, angels came and ministered unto him" (Matthew 4:11). It was the sword of the Lord, the Word of God (Ephesians 6:17), that rendered the devil helpless and powerless. *"He will flee"* is promised to those that resist the devil. He has to go and take his darkness with Him. He cannot stand strong very long around a group of praying women who are filled with the Word of God and the Spirit, and who know how to pray the Word and allow the Spirit to be in control!

Jesus said to bind! Matthew 16:19 says, "And I will give unto thee the keys of the kingdom of heaven: and whatsoever thou shalt bind on earth shall be bound in heaven: and whatsoever thou shalt loose on earth shall be loosed in heaven."

Jesus was giving the *church* the power to bind and loose. He gave them a key which was a badge of power or authority. The power of binding and loosing is to be shared by all believers. Jesus talks about this in Matthew 18:18-19:

Verily I say unto you, Whatsoever ye shall bind on earth, shall be bound in heaven: and whatsoever ye shall loose on earth shall be loosed in heaven. Again I say unto you, That if two of you shall agree on earth as touching any thing that they shall ask, it shall be done for them of my Father which is in heaven.

The *prayer of agreement* is a powerful tool in spiritual warfare.

In Mark 16, Jesus promised that signs would follow the believer. Those signs included casting out devils and evil spirits and also that the sick would be healed. It is a promise!

II Timothy 1:7 tells about one of those evil spirits: "For God hath not given us the spirit of fear; but of power, and of love, and of a sound mind." The spirit of fear can be spoken to and commanded to leave. The best way to speak to it is to pray the Word over it. When that spirit hears, "It is written," it has to leave!

Satan wants to put fear on women and get the upper hand in their lives and the lives of their families. Just as the devil tempted Jesus, he will also tempt the women of this generation, but they can win against him, just as Jesus did. Spurgeon explains it in the following words:

Temptation vanishes before a sight of the dying Redeemer. Then inbred lust roars against us, and we overcome it through the blood of the Lamb, for "the blood of Jesus Christ, His Son, cleanseth us from all sin." Sometimes a raging corruption or a strong habit wars upon us, and then we conquer by the might of the sanctifying Spirit of God, who is with us and shall be in us evermore. Or else it is the world which tempts, and our feet have almost gone; but we overcome the world through the victory of faith.

If Satan raises against us the lust of the flesh, the lust of the eye and the pride of life, all at once, we are still delivered, for the Lord is a wall of fire round about us. The inward life bravely resists all sin, and God's help is given to believers to preserve them from all evil in the moment of urgent need; even as he helped His martyrs and confessors to speak the right word when called unprepared to confront their adversaries. Care not, therefore, O thou truster in the Lord Jesus, how fierce thine enemy may be on this day! As young David slew the lion and the bear and smote the Philistines, even so shalt thou go from victory to victory. [5]

It is possible to slay the enemy and fight against the evil forces of hell through the power of prayer. Years ago an unknown woman wrote the following article in *The Pentecostal Evangel* about an incident her family experienced during World War II, which shows the power to reverse evil:

Back of our home in the Philippines during World War II was the place where the Japanese tortured and killed their victims. We could hear the screams of the tortured day and night. They liked to throw the babies in the air and catch them on the point of a sword, and the things they devised to torture adults were unthinkable.

Twice my father had been taken by enemy officers and had been returned to us as a result of my mother's prayers. The third time the officer said, "He has been returned to you two times—but don't you ever think he will be spared the third time. This time he dies."

"If you don't believe in prayer, get out of here," Mother told him.

The officer left, taking my father with him.

Mother put us five children to bed on our grass mats. Then she began her prayer vigil in behalf of our father. At four a.m., she woke us saying, "The burden has become so heavy I cannot bear it alone. Get up and help me pray for your father."

We gathered in a circle around Mother, with the two-month-old baby on the floor in the center. While we were praying we heard footsteps. We were sure the officer was coming for us, and Mother threw her arms around us as far as she could reach.

Suddenly she said, "Those are your father's footsteps!

"Are you safe?" he asked, pulling the bamboo door back. We lit the lamp and saw his white shirt splattered with blood from those who had stood near him.

"I understand now why they let me go," he said soberly. "You were praying."

He told us that he had been the last in a row of ten men. A man had gone down the row, slashing off the heads of each with a sword.

"He raised his sword when he came to me, and just as he was ready to bring it down the officer in charge suddenly screamed, 'Stop!' Then that officer roared at me, 'Go home. Quick, get out of here. Go home.'

"Then he dived at me, grabbed my arm and propelled me toward the gate and past the guard as fast as he could—and here I am."

That had been what was happening at the time Mother was so burdened that she got us up to pray. We do not know what the officer experienced to make him change the order—but we do know why. 6

Prayer such as this has an unshakable power, for when women begin to pray hot, fervent prayers, immediately heaven is on the alert. God and His angels are watching, listening, and recording her heart's cry. "For the eyes of the Lord are over the righteous, and his ears are open unto their prayers" (I Peter 3:12).

Every prayer a woman prays is being stored in golden vials. "And when he had taken the book, the four beasts and four and twenty elders fell down before the Lamb, having every one of them harps, and golden vials full of odours, which are the prayers of saints" (Revelation 5:8).

"...that he should offer it with the prayers of all saints upon the golden altar which was before the throne. And the smoke of the incense, which came with the prayers of the saints, ascended up before God out of the angel's hand" (Revelation 8:3-4).

This book is an urgent call for women everywhere to begin to pray fervent prayers! May the odor of their prayers become as an ocean of incense before the throne of God.

Before this chapter can close, it must take the reader to a very graphic picture of spiritual warfare. The story is given in Daniel 10. Daniel had been praying and fasting for 21 days when suddenly an angel visited him. It was not a calm, laid-back visit, but it was earth-shaking. Standing by the Hiddekel River, Daniel lifted up his eyes and saw a man clothed in white linen, girded with fine gold. "His body also was like the beryl, and his face as the appearance of lightning, and his eyes as lamps of fire, and his arms and his feet like in colour to polished brass, and the voice of his words like the voice of a multitude" (Daniel 10:6).

The men that were with Daniel did not see the angel—only Daniel was allowed to see him—but their bodies began to quake and shake so that they ran to hide themselves. When Daniel was left alone, He found himself with his face toward the ground, in a deep sleep, with no strength left in him. The angel touched him, set him upon his knees and the following occured:

And he said unto me, O Daniel, a man greatly beloved, understand the words that I speak unto thee, and stand upright: for unto thee am I now sent. And when he had spoken this word unto me, I stood trembling. Then said he unto me, Fear not, Daniel: for from the first day that thou didst set thine heart to understand, and to chasten thyself before thy God, thy words were heard, and I am come for thy words (Daniel 10:11-12).

Notice what is happening here. The angel is going to tell Daniel about the opposition to his prayers, the power of darkness that was unveiled. He said, "But the prince of the kingdom of Persia withstood me one and twenty days: but, lo, Michael, one of the chief princes, came to help me; and I remained there with the kings of Persia" (Daniel 10:13).

The picture portrays Daniel praying and fasting. His prayers went up to God's throne. God sent an angel down with the answer, but on the way the angel had to war with the prince of Persia, one of the princes of the *unseen world of evil*. The power of darkness was so strong, that God sent Michael, the great warring angel, to help the other angel in the conflict. After the two angels subdued the prince of Persia, the first angel was able to deliver the message.

The angel did not just deliver a message, but he strengthened Daniel.

"Then there came again and touched me one like the appearance of a man, and he strengthened me. And said, O man greatly beloved, fear not: peace be unto thee, be strong, yea, be strong. And when he had spoken unto me, I was strengthened, and said, Let my lord speak; for thou hast strengthened me" (Daniel 10:18-19).

There is definitely an *unseen* world that is working against us, but there is also another *unseen* world which is working for us. We are able to conquer through the mighty power of God!

"Prayer is not overcoming God's reluctance, it is laying hold of His highest willingness."

Archbishop Trench [1]

8
Expect Results

It is important to reiterate a truth to awaken women to greater expectation: Our God has boundless resources. The only limit is in us. Our asking, our thinking, our praying are too small. Our expectations are too limited.

The following account is one of my favorite stories. It depicts a woman who prayed through the night and then believed that God would answer her prayer, and He did!

Once there was a man who owned a little grocery store on the West side of town. It was the week before Christmas after the World War. A tired looking woman came into the store and asked him for enough food to make up a Christmas dinner for her children. He asked her how much she could afford to spend.

She answered, "My husband was killed in the war. I have nothing to offer but a little prayer."

The man was not very sentimental and felt that a grocery store could not be run like a bread line, so he said to her, "Write it on paper," and turned about his business.

To his surprise, the woman plucked a piece of paper out of her bosom and handed it to him over the counter and said, "I did that during the night watching over my sick baby."

The grocer took the paper before he could recover from his surprise, and then regretted having done so. For what would he do with it, what could he say? Then an idea suddenly came to him. He placed the paper, without even reading it, on the weight side of his old-fashioned scales. He said, "We shall see how much food this is worth."

To his astonishment the scale would not go down when he put a loaf of bread on the other side. To his confusion and embarrassment, it would not go down though he kept on adding food, anything he could lay his hands on quickly, because people were watching him.

He tried to be gruff but he was making a bad job of it. His face got red and it made him angry to be flustered. So finally he said, "Well, that's all the scales will hold anyway. Here's a bag. You'll have to put it in yourself. I'm busy."

With what sounded like a gasp or a little sob, she took the bag and started packing in the food, wiping her eyes on her sleeves every time her arm was free to do so. He tried not to look, but he could not help seeing that he had given her a pretty big bag and that it was not quite full. So he tossed a large cheese down the counter, but he did not say anything, nor did he see the timid smile of grateful understanding which glistened in her moist eyes at this final betrayal of the grocer's crusty exterior.

When the woman had gone, he went to look at the scales, scratching his head and shaking it in puzzlement. Then he found the solution. The scales were broken. The grocer never saw the woman again, but for the rest of his life he remembered her better than any other woman and thought of her often.

He knew it had not been just his imagination, for he still had the slip of paper upon which the woman's prayer had been written, "Please Lord, give us this day our daily bread" (Matthew 6:11).

Scales that were working the minute before, suddenly broke, all because of a woman's prayer of faith.

That needy woman went to that particular store believing that God would take care of her, and He did!

There is power in belief. Her belief became a fire that helped her accomplish that which she had set out to do. She believed, so she received!

The promise is given in Psalm 37:4: "Delight thyself also in the Lord; and He shall give thee the desires of thine heart." It is a promise! It must be believed! Those who pray and delight in God will receive the desire of their heart.

The story is told about a pastor who preached one morning from Matthew 18:19: "If two of you shall agree on earth as touching any thing that they shall ask, it shall be done for them of my Father which is in heaven." After he read his text, the pastor asked the question, "Do you believe it?" Of course he did not expect an answer, but one was forthcoming. As he paused for a moment that his question might be understood, a very poor member of the congregation, poor in this world's goods but rich in faith, rose to her feet. "I believe it, Pastor," she said, "And I want you to claim that promise with me."

The pastor was staggered. He did not feel like he had the faith to claim the promise, and as he hesitated, a big burly blacksmith in the congregation rose to his feet. "I'll claim that promise with you, Auntie," he said, and together the two, the poor washer-woman and the blacksmith, dropped to their knees in the aisle and poured out their hearts in prayer for the salvation of the woman's husband.

Now it happened that this man was a riverboat captain on the Rio Grande, a swearing, foul-mouthed drunken sot, and he was at that moment sleeping off a drunk at home.

That night, for the first time in many years at least, the old riverboat captain was in the church and while the pastor preached the woman prayed, not for the salvation of her husband, rather she was thanking God for it, for she seemed to know it would happen that night.

When the invitation was given, this foul-mouthed captain came to give his heart to the Lord, and became one of the most dependable and faithful workers in that church.

It only takes faith the size of a grain of mustard seed to receive a miracle. Jesus said all it takes is belief in God. Mark 11:22 says, "And Jesus answering saith unto them, Have faith in God."

It is simply *belief* that gets an answer. Matthew 21:22 says, "And all things, whatsoever ye shall ask in prayer, believing, ye shall receive." Once when Jesus heard that a little girl whom He had been asked to pray for was dead, He said to her father, "Be not afraid, only believe" (Mark 5:36).

Faith is believing in God when there is nothing *seen* in which to believe. It is believing only God's Word instead of facts, feelings or that which is seen. It is impossible to have this kind of faith unless you become as a little child. Jesus said, "Verily I say unto you, Except ye be converted, and become as little children, ye shall not enter into the kingdom of heaven" (Matthew 18:3).

Small children, who have not been abused, but live a normal life with their needs met and who have experienced love, will believe anything an adult tells them. They hang onto every word. They are eager to believe, and respond with trust and faith.

This characteristic is essential to a prayer meeting. There must be childlike faith to believe that God will hear and answer prayer and wants to do good things for His children. It is His good pleasure to give. "Fear not, little flock; for it is your Father's good pleasure to give you the kingdom" (Luke 12:32).

When Jesus taught the multitudes how to pray, He ended it with basically the same statement as in Luke 12:32. "Ask, and it shall be given you; seek, and ye shall find; knock, and it shall be opened unto you: If ye then, being evil, know how to give good gifts unto your children, how much more shall your Father which is in heaven give good things to them that ask him?" (Matthew 7:7, 11).

It is His *good* pleasure to give *good* things to them that ask. He wants to do it as the following scriptures depict:

"O taste and see that the Lord is good: blessed is the man that trusteth in him. The young lions do lack, and suffer hunger: but they that seek the Lord shall not want any *good* thing" (Psalm 34:8, 10).

"For the Lord God is a sun and shield: the Lord will give grace and glory: no *good* thing will he withhold from them that walk uprightly" (Psalm 84:11).

It is a promise: they shall not want *any good thing*, and *no good thing* will He withhold from those that seek after Him.

"Groanings which cannot be uttered are often prayers which cannot be refused."

Charles H. Spurgeon [1]

9
Intercessory Prayer

INTERCESSORS TOUCH MANY LIVES THROUGH THEIR PRAYERS

Because you prayed—
God touched our weary bodies with His power
And gave us strength for many a trying hour
In which we might have faltered, had not you,
Our intercessors faithful been, and true.

Because you prayed—
God touched our lips with coals from altar fire,
Gave Spirit-fulness, and did so inspire
That, when we spoke, sin-blinded souls did see;
Sin's chains were broken;
Captives were made free.

Because you prayed—
The dwellers in the dark have found the Light;
The glad good-news has banished heathen night;
The message of the Cross, so long delayed,
Has brought them life at last—
Because you prayed.

Charles B. Bowser

Intercessory prayer is praying in behalf of someone else. It is making supplication with urgency. Women are naturally burden-bearers. They care about others, they live for others and are always doing things that involve helping others. So it is natural for them to pray for the needs of others.

Praying for others is important and it has powerful effects, but usually at a prayer meeting the prayers are for many needs. Because of the time involved and the number of needs presented, the time spent on each prayer is rather short.

That is why it is necessary for me to insert here, that as much as I advocate women coming together and praying together, there are some prayers that can only be prayed while alone. I call these *strong* prayers. Jesus prayed this type of prayer in the garden of Gethsemane. "And being in an agony he prayed more earnestly: and his sweat was as it were great drops of blood falling down to the ground" (Luke 22:44). Jesus took Peter, James and John with Him apart from the other disciples, but then He left them and went alone to pray.

Sometimes the intercessor will feel as if she is birthing something. There will be strong tears and heart-wrenching sobs, and even the body will feel the wrestling like struggle. A woman facing a natural birth is pretty much alone. She does not want the whole world watching her birth a baby. It is the same in birthing something in the spiritual. Some prayers can only be prayed alone.

It is the "I will not let you go," prayer that brings results, as was in the case of Jacob. Alone on a dark night, he wrestled with an angel until the breaking of the day. Finally the angel said, "Let me go, for the day breaketh, And he said, I will not let thee go, except thou bless me" (Genesis 32:26).

Did he get what he was wrestling for? Yes! "And he said, thy name shall be called no more Jacob, but Israel: for as a prince hast thou power with God and with men, and hast prevailed...And he blessed him there" (Genesis 32:28-29). Notice that he received his answer because he prevailed.

I have been a minister's wife for over 37 years and there have been times, I have prayed this type of prevailing prayer. These wrestling prayers have usually been when I was alone with God. Oh, the wrestling, the sobbing, the birthing, the anguish and the warring, but this kind of praying always gets an answer!

When women prevail and wrestle in prayer they gain power with God and man, just as Jacob did. They walk in a new dimension. They are truly blessed women. Not only are they a blessing, but they receive a blessing. God seems to smile on those who will pray and travail for needs. Wrestling prayer is not in vain; it accomplishes great things.

WRESTLING PRAYER CHANGES THINGS

Wrestling prayer can wonders do,
Bring relief in deepest straits:
Prayer can force a passage through
Iron bars and brazen gates.
Author unknown

This literally happened shortly after the ascension of Jesus. When the new doctrine of Jesus was being preached in and around Jerusalem, the governmental leaders became afraid of an insurrection. Thus, King Herod ordered the death of one of the leaders of the new church, James the Apostle. After James' death, Herod then arrested Peter and placed him in prison. But something took place that changed the king's orders. The church gathered together at the house·of Mary, the mother of John Mark, and began to pray. "Peter therefore was kept in prison: but prayer was made without ceasing of the church unto God for him" (Acts 12:5).

Peter was sleeping between two soldiers, bound with two chains, and a light shined in the prison. While they were praying, an angel appeared to him. The angel touched Peter on the side, raised him up, and told him to arise quickly. Then the chains fell off his hands and the angel said, "Gird thyself, and bind on thy sandals. And so he did. And he saith unto him, Cast thy garment about thee, and follow me" (Acts 12:8).

Peter followed the angel and thought he was seeing a vision while passing through the first and second ward. Then when he came to the iron gate which led into the city,

174

and it opened by itself, and the angel had departed, he came to himself and said, "Now I know of a surety, that the Lord hath sent his angel, and hath delivered me out of the hand of Herod" (Acts 12:11).

Peter hurried to Mary's house where many were gathered together praying. He then knocked at the door of the gate, which was opened by a young girl named Rhoda. When she heard Peter's voice, she did not open the gate, but shut the door and ran inside and told everyone that Peter was outside. They could not believe what they were hearing. "And they said unto her, Thou art mad. But she constantly affirmed that it was even so. Then said they, It is his angel" (Acts 12:15).

Peter just kept knocking and finally they went to the door of the gate and opened it. They were all astonished at what God had done. God was merciful to them even with their seeming lack of faith.

Wrestling prayer is unceasing prayer for special personal needs or the needs of others until an answer comes. It can also be a special time of prayer when the Spirit prays through a person for someone else, as shown in the following story, which tells how a woman began to pray intercessory prayer for the author, Rev. Richard M. Davis:

> The pain had intensified for two years. From an occasional annoying tingle in my left knee, the pain had increased in frequency and intensity....I tried to have faith that God would intervene. Nonetheless, when the pain continued at an intolerable level, I resorted to aspirin and pain relievers to endure the

pain. Even during the night I would awaken in such pain I could not sleep. Night after night I would arise to take medication.

I was becoming alarmed. The amount of aspirin being consumed could not possibly be healthy. I had not had a restful night for months. My personal life was suffering as well as the areas of my involvement in the ministry. My thinking was not clear and concise. I was fuzzy and lacked concentration. The pain was radiating from the knee into my lower back. It had reached a level of intensity that caused me often to drag my left leg behind me until the medication could take effect.

I began to seek professional medical help. It was several months and physicians later before a definite diagnosis was completed. One doctor had noticed in the X-rays a congenital birth defect in the lower back. He stated that the problem was there to stay and prescribed an anti-inflammatory drug to reduce the pain...After suffering with the problem for two years, I accepted it as a routine of life. Healing was far from my conscious thought. Then it happened, suddenly and without warning!

The local church was having a twenty-four hour prayer chain, and I selected 5 o'clock to 6 o'clock in the morning. God always seemed to bless me in a special way in those early hours.

The prayer time was going well. Nothing phenomenal was happening, but the presence of God was very near every morning. There were a half dozen or so praying during that particular hour.

One morning toward the end of the week, I was praying on my knees. During the entire week I had not asked for healing one time. I prayed for our missionaries, lost loved ones, and revival around the world. But suddenly a dear saint in prayer began to travail. It was an urgent, wailing spirit of travail and intercession.

At that precise moment God knocked me from my knees to my back onto the floor. I continued to pray and worship. I did not know what the dear sister was travailing for, but I knew that God was healing me at that very moment. I just worshipped and thanked God for my healing.

I left the church that morning with a real sense of victory and power. I felt on top of everything. There was only one problem. I was still on medication for my back. I was afraid to stop the medication. I had tried to stop many times, but in only a few hours I would hurt so badly...It was two days before the victory came.

"Lord," I cried, "I'm tired of living under fear. I am going to trust You!"

And with that I laid my medicine aside. I never took another pill from that point forward. Four hours passed, but there was no pain. Six hours went by and still there was victory.

The hours slipped into days, the days turned into weeks. Seven months have passed, and I am free from pain. I can lift up anything I desire. I sleep well at night. The pain has disappeared forever. God healed my back. 2

Intercessory prayer is standing in the gap for another. The first mention of someone interceding for another is found in the first book of the Bible. Genesis 18 tells a story that depicts the mercy of God and His desire to commune with mankind. The Lord talked to Abraham and told him that He was going to destroy Sodom and Gomorrah because their sin was very grievous.

"And Abraham drew near, and said, Wilt thou also destroy the righteous with the wicked? Peradventure there be fifty righteous within the city: wilt thou also destroy and not spare the place for the fifty righteous that are therein?" (Genesis 18:23-24).

The Lord answered Abraham back and told him that if He could find fifty righteous, He would not destroy the city. Abraham started thinking of who was righteous and had a difficult time coming up with fifty names, so he asked God to spare the city for forty-five righteous. This went on until they reached the number of ten righteous. There were not even ten, so God, for Abraham's sake, said He would save Lot and his family.

God is merciful and listens when someone intercedes for another. He proved this over and over in the case of Moses and the children of Israel. The people would sin and God would want to destroy them. Then Moses would intercede for his people, and God would repent of what He had decided to do. An example of this is the time when the children of Israel, under the leadership of Aaron, had made a golden calf to worship. Meanwhile Moses was on Mount Sinai receiving the tablets given to him by God, which contained the Ten Commandments. God said, "Now therefore let me alone, that my wrath may wax hot against them, and that I may consume them: and I will make of thee a great nation" (Exodus 32:10).

Moses began to act as an intercessor for the people, asking the Lord not to do what He wanted to do to them, and God honored Moses' prayer. "And the Lord repented of the evil which he thought to do unto his people" (Exodus 32:14).

God listens to His **children pray**. **If they are seeking** after God and trying to follow His precepts, He goes out of His way to help them when they call upon Him. Intercessory prayer does not only bring deliverance, healing and miracles, but it also opens doors for those prayed for, and locks out the forces of the enemy. Jean Paul Richter said it like this: "Let prayer be the key of the day and the bolt of the night." 3

A mother can pray and intercede for the salvation of her children to such an extent that her prayers will follow and affect them wherever they go. The following story, found in an old book, proves this and exemplifies the power of a mother's prayer.

At one time eight young law students were going out to spend the Sabbath riotously. They had a deck of cards in one hip pocket and a flask of wine in the other. At ten o'clock, as they were going down the road to their loitering places, the church bell rang, and one fellow stopped and said: "Fellows, I am going back. I am going to church and Sunday school." One hilarious chap gave him the horselaugh and said: "Oh, Jim, come on out of that nonsense, quit sissying around about going to Sunday school. Get in this gang and be a good sport." But Jim said: "No, I am going back." The ring leaders came up and took hold of the boy and said, "Here, quit that nonsense, or we will throw you into the river; we will baptize you right. Come on," and they were going to force him. He said, "Hold on, fellows, I know that you are big and strong enough, seven against one, to throw me into the river, but before you do so, I want to tell you a story. Three months ago, when I was about to leave home, my invalid mother called me to her bedside. She has been an invalid all my life, for she nearly gave her life when she gave me birth. I can never remember seeing her walk. She said, 'Son, you are going away from home to study law, and your father hasn't means to pay your way, so that you can't come back to visit. I am failing rapidly, Jim, and this is probably the last time you will ever see me in this world. I would like to have you come and kneel by my bedside while I lay my hands on your head and breathe my heart out to God in prayer.' I kneeled by my mother's bedside, fellows, and she prayed a prayer that the angels wrote upon the tablet of my heart. I could repeat it word for word. She asked God to help me to be a great, useful man. When I arose, I took her thin, white hands in mine, and I said, 'Mother, what can I do for you?' and with her eyes suffused with tears of love, she said, 'Son, you can do just one thing for me. Just remember, that every Sabbath morning, as long as your mother lives, between the hours of ten and eleven o'clock, she is going to be praying for you, praying that God may make you a true, useful man.' When that bell rang, fellows, I knew it was the hour my mother was to be in prayer for me, and right now she is praying for me. Fellows, I am going back to church and Sunday school. I am going to be a real man." As he turned on his heel, the young fellow that had given him the horse laugh, turned to hide a tear, for he remembered how his mother was praying for him; and the ring leaders who had threatened to throw him into the river, turned to hide their faces in shame, for they, too, remembered how in the hills back home, mothers were praying for them. As the lad started back to Sunday school every last one of the seven followed silently on behind. Within three weeks all eight of those young men had become converted, and gave their hearts and lives to God, and all went out to live great Christian lives, and bless the world with high service, and why? Because of mother's prayer.

Prayer is the mightiest power in the world. If I could have the ears of all the mothers of America, and I could give them but one message, I would say, "Mothers of America, remember that prayer is the mightiest force that you have in all this world." Prayer beautifies a mother's life as nothing else can do. Prayer gives guidance to a mother's life amid her perplexities, as nothing else can do. Prayer empowers a mother's life for her many duties as nothing else can do. Her prayer is the agency through which the mother can distribute blessings to her children far or near, as nothing else can do. Prayer is the supreme agency in the building of the lives of the men of tomorrow. [4]

Although it seems impossible, the same prayer power that worked for those mothers over 75 years ago is still as powerful today. It is a different world, a different set of circumstances, but the same God! Women can make war against the enemy of the souls of her children and win.

Would to God that more mothers around the world would begin to pray for their children. There is nothing more formidable than a praying mother who walks close to her God. She will always win! Hell must release the hold on her children; it has no choice, "For with God nothing shall be impossible" (Luke 1:37).

"Faith sees the invisible, believes the incredible, and receives the impossible."

10
Praying Women Receive Miracles

The live prayer hour on the radio has been mentioned in the Foreword and elsewhere in this book. This chapter will highlight a few of the miracles and answers to prayer that God gave us in 1998. We have record of 419 praise reports. We know there are more; they are just not reported. There were 21 deliverances, 35 salvations, 160 financial blessings, 121 physical healings, 16 marriages restored, and 66 miscellaneous miracles, which included runaway children returning home, God intervening in court cases and one kidnapping victim found safe.

Out of the 419 miracles or answers to prayer, the following ones were chosen to share with you and are broken down according to subject:

HEALINGS

February 25: Two-year-old Adam Haugh received a miraculous recovery after prayer. Recovered from two surgeries yesterday: playing, eating, has no fever, or pain.

March 18: Stephani called in on March 11. Jarrod was in a bad accident—not expected to live. She called in and reported that the doctors could not find the blood clots that had threatened his life. God dissolved them.

May 6: Debra called in with a praise report. Doctor found a lump in her breast. She called for prayer, then went back in to the doctor and he couldn't find it. He was very puzzled.

May 6: Bonnie healed of a brain tumor. When they went to do the scan before surgery, it was gone!

June 10: Prayed two weeks ago for seven-month-old Anthony for seizures. Went to Kaiser after prayer and they found nothing wrong with Anthony—seizures are gone.

July 15: Gloria called a year ago asking for prayer for a tumor. The doctor cannot find the tumor. It is gone!

July 22: John healed of blindness from diabetic condition. The eye-sight came back—doctor is amazed!

July 29: Dave walking and talking—out of coma for one month after being pinned down by a 16,000-ton generator.

August 5: After prayer Rosie went in for a colon test and they found no sign of cancer, which they feared was there.

August12: It was feared that Olivia had cancer in her uterus. After prayer—the test result came back: *no cancer*.

August 26: Roberta called in with prayer need on August 19. She was in a car accident, with a broken hip, and seven months pregnant. One week later, after prayer, the doctors sent her home on August 25th, and gave her permission to walk with a walker. Received another praise report on November 18, 1998: She delivered a 9 lb. baby boy. All went well.

August 26: Received a praise report concerning three-year-old Denny Crow, whose head was run over by the front tire of a 3/4 ton pick-up and his chest by the back tire. One half-hour after prayer was requested, Danny was awakened telling his mom he loved her. September 2, another praise report was called in: "The healing of his bones and skull is miraculously from God." In December 1998, we received a picture of Dennis, Katrin and Denny Crow, taken two months after Denny was run over. The picture was accompanied by these words: "At UC Davis, God healed Denny's pancreas. The MRI showed it cut in two pieces. When the doctor went in to do surgery, it was healed! Even the doctor said God got there first. Later that night we were told Denny was brain dead...Wrong! The doctors said he'd be in ICU for 3 to 5 weeks. He was home in 5 weeks. Praise be to our God!"

September 16: Diana healed of lung cancer.

September 16: Two weeks ago, a request was called in for Maria Garcia who had congestive heart failure, on ventilation, and not expected to live. She is now home getting stronger and the family is now going to church.

October 7: Diane healed of colon cancer.

October 24: Jackie Phillips called in for daughter, Jenny, who was healed of joint pain after three weeks of prayer. Daughter was on crutches and in a wheel-chair. She was completely healed—doctors said it was rare virus in joints.

December 9: Three-year-old Michael was healed of cystic fibrosis. Michael had five positive tests for cystic fibrosis.

After prayer, he had two negative DNA tests—family is thankful for prayer!

December16: Gail Alexander healed of liver cancer.

MARRIAGES RESTORED

August 5: Jim sent in request every week for over one year. It looked impossible, but God is finally restoring their marriage.

August 26: Beverly had previously called in and asked prayer for her husband's salvation and restoration of marriage. He had moved out of the home. God answered! Her husband called home and asked her for forgiveness and wants to work on the marriage. She said when she called in: "When you are on the bottom, look up. God can do the IMPOSSIBLE!"

October 18: Mike had called in because his wife had told him she was going to leave him. Since prayer was made, she has changed her mind and says not she is not leaving.

FINANCIAL BLESSINGS

January 1: Fredonnia reported that after prayer was made, a $5,000.00 medical bill was mysteriously paid in full!

January 21: Elizabeth Wong had called on January 7, for God to provide her money to pay medical bills, a house to rent or buy, and to give her a financial blessing. She found a house three days later to buy. Her father is loaning the whole amount to her ($65,000.00), because it is such a great deal. "God has come through in a mighty way. Wow! Thank you Jesus," she says.

February 4: Josephine called in and reported that after prayer was made, their house is not in foreclosure anymore.

June 10: Sherre called in and asked for prayer that God would send their SSI check. The very next day after prayer, they received their check.

July 22: Jennifer needed money desperately. After prayer, she received $1,000.00 "out of the blue."

July 29: Kim Sarale shared a praise report. They needed money for their moving expenses to a new house. God answered three ways: Her husband was blessed with a bonus check for $645.00. Her husband's dad bought them a new refrigerator. The company they were buying their home from was only supposed to spend $4,000.00 on the termite work. However, now they are spending $5,700.00 and doing a lot of cosmetic work on the house.

July 29: Bob called in with a praise report. He was told that it would cost $300 to fix car, after prayer was made, found that it was only a loose wire and paid nothing.

August 12: Trina called last Wednesday regarding IRS payment they said she owed. After prayer, IRS found out computer had made a mistake—do not owe a penny!

September 28: Millie Boren writes: "Glory to Jesus. Received debt cancellation. Delivered from financial bondage, and am living according to Mark 11:22-24."

November 4: Charlotte called in with a praise report. We had prayed that God would supply her with some new dining room furniture. God sent them a new dinette set, no longer eating on the floor.

December 2: After prayer, Lisa received first job in 15 years.

December 9: Susie stepped out in faith during KCJH Family Reunion to pledge to the station. She asked prayer for financial help. God has now tripled her salary and has given her weekends off.

December 9: After prayer Debbie received truckload of wood to heat home.

December 9: Edna called in this praise report: "Blessed with a car on Thanksgiving morning, received new carpet on December 7, and received a full-time job. Praise God!"

December 16: Mary needed money for Christmas and asked that we would pray she would not be alone on Christmas. She called in and said that she has sold several items at a garage sale and has been invited to spend Christmas with a family—she will not be alone.

DELIVERANCES

January 13: Barbara was delivered from depression.

January 20: Christina was delivered from the strongholds of the mind and uplifted by the message that was given during the prayer hour. She felt like it was just for her— straight from God.

February 4: Praise report: Salvation for Kim and deliverance from heroin addiction.

June 3: Jeremy and Mindy both delivered from drugs, and they both got a job.

September 2: Jo delivered from smoking. She also had prayer for her daughter Amy to return home. She came home last Wednesday. Praise God!

September 16: Mike was delivered from witchcraft. He had left home four years ago. Had a nice conversation with mom—is being restored back to his family.

September 30: Sandy's mind has been healed. She has made a turn around in her life to serve God, and has been delivered from drugs and alcohol.

November 11: Marty was delivered from anger and rebellion. Mother was able to speak to him just hours after prayer went up.

December 30: Dave is thanking God that he has been delivered from alcoholism

MISCELLANEOUS

March 6: Tiffany ran away from home for seven months. After prayer was made, she moved back home.

May 20: Christina ran away from home four years ago. After prayer, she came home safe.

May 27: Sally's son called after prayer was made—had not heard from him in six months.

June 17: Nathan had been wrongfully accused of a serious crime. When he walked into the courtroom, the accuser stood up immediately and said, "He is not the one." Nathan raised his hands in open court and shouted, "Praise God!"

September 16: Angie got her kids for full custody—been waiting for four years.

September 30: Anna, who had run away from home, returned home after prayer.

November 4: Dee waited for one year for child custody. After prayer, court granted her daughter to her.

Many wonderful things happen when women pray and believe. Even now, as this book is being prepared, there are more miracles and answers to prayer being reported as a result of women praying together and binding the forces of hell.

Won't you become a part of the many prayer warriors that are springing up around the globe? As we enter a new millennium, it is time to pray with new fervency and power, to take authority over the enemy and take back some things that he has stolen from our families and churches.

We can pray and make hell tremble, as Chrysostom, one of the most beloved and celebrated of the fathers of the early Christian Church, so ably recorded it: "The *potency of prayer* hath subdued the strength of fire; it hath bridled the rage of lions, hushed anarchy to rest, extinguished wars, appeased the elements, expelled demons, burst the chains of death, expanded the gates of heaven, assuaged diseases, repelled frauds, rescued cities from destruction, stayed the sun in its course, and arrested the progress of the thunderbolt. Prayer is an all-sufficient panoply, a treasure undiminished, a mine which is never exhausted, a sky unobscured by clouds, a heaven unruffled by the storm. It is the root, the fountain, the mother, of a thousand blessings." [1]

EPILOGUE

I received the following message from Freddi Trammel on March 12, 1997 at 5:45 in the morning. She found it in an old book and the Lord impressed her to give it to me. At the time I was in the middle of a difficult trial.

As she read it to me, tears ran down my face and dripped into my lap. May they also help you to keep your gaze toward heaven in prayer.

Set your gaze toward heaven. Your eyes shall behold my glory, for I have brought you through the testing time and my heart rejoices over you.

You see but a part of the picture, but I see the design in its completion. You cannot know what is in my mind and what I am creating with the material of thy life. Only be thou yielded in my hands. Thou needest not make thine own plans for I am in control, and thou wouldst bring disaster by interference, even as a child, who would wish to help a master artist and with untrained use of the brush would ruin the canvas.

So rest thy soul—this knowing that I have been at work, and in ways thou hast least suspected, for the picture and the work with which I was engaged were entirely different.

I make no idle strokes. What I do is never haphazard. My every move is one of vital creativity. And every stroke is part of the whole.

Never be alarmed by a sudden dash of color seemingly out of context. Say only in thy questioning heart, "It is the Infinite wielding His brush. Surely He doeth all things well. He can stand back and view His work and say, "It is good."

Notes

Preface
[1] Knight, Walter B., *Knight's Treasure of Illustrations*, (Wm. B. Eerdmans Publishing Co., Grand Rapids, MI: 1963), p. 266.
[2] Ravenhill, Leonard, *Why Revival Tarries*, (Bethany Fellowship, Minneapolis, MN: 1959), p. 81.

Chapter 1
[1] Johnson, Joseph S., *A Field of Diamonds*, (Broadman Press, Nashville, TN: 1974), p. 153.
[2] Lockyer, Dr. Herbert, *The Women of the Bible*, (Zondervan Publishing House, Grand Rapids, MI: 1967), p. 13.
[3] Ibid., p. 13-14.
[4] Tan, Paul Lee, ThD., (Assurance Publishers, Rockville, Maryland: 1979), #4583.
[5] Ibid., #3671
[6] Ibid., #3678
[7] Ibid., #4656.
[8] Cowman, Mrs. Charles E., *Streams in the Desert Vol. 2*, (Zondervan Publishing House, Grand Rapids, MI: 1966), May 15.
[9] Ibid., November 6.

Chapter 2
[1] Johnson, p. 156.
[2] Knights, p. 267.
[3] S. I. McMillen, M.D., *None of These Diseases*, (Fleming H. Revell Co., Westwood, NJ: 1963), p. 99.
[4] Knight, p. 266.
[5] Ibid.
[6] Demoss, Arthur and Nancy, *The Gold Star Family Album*, Fleming H. Revell Co., Old Tappan, NJ: 1968), p. 139.
[7] Tan, #3904.
[8] Knight, 265.
[9] Ibid., p. 262.

[10] McMillen, p. 147.
[11] Ibid., p. 144.
[12] Knight, p. 262.
[13] Ibid.
[14] Ibid, p. 264.
[15] Cowman, November 10.
[16] Lockyer, 101.
[17] Tan, #2829.
[18] Johnson, p. 156.
[19] Knight, p. 275.
[20] Haney, Joy, *His Angels*, (Guideposts, New York, NY: 1998), pp. 21-23.
[21] Johnson, p. 114.

Chapter 3
[1] Johnson, p. 153.
[2] Knight, p. 32.

Chapter 4
[1] Charles G. Finney and L. G. Parkhurst, Jr.*Principles of Prayer,* (Bethany House Publishers, Minneapolis, MN: 1980) p. 17.
[2] Tan, #391.
[3] Ibid., #419.
[4] Ibid., #419.
[5] Ibid., #1922.
[6] Knight, p. 202.
[7] Lockyer, p. 66.
[8] Johnson, p. 150.
[9] Cowman, June 8.
[10] Johnson, p. 156.
[11] Wallace, Mary H., *God Answers Prayer,* (Word Aflame Press, Hazelwood, MO: 1986), pp. 135-139.

Chapter 5
[1] Ravenhill, p. 156.
[2] Tan, #419.

Chapter 6
[1] Knight, p. 266.

[2] Howell, Clinton T., *Lines to Live By*, (Thomas Nelson, Inc., Nashville, TN: 1972), p. 29.

[3] Edman, V. Raymond, *They Found the Secret,* (Zondervan Publishing House, Grand Rapids, Michigan: 1963), p.41.

[4] Hobe, Phyllis, *Dawnings, Finding God's Light in the Darkness,* (Guideposts, Carmel, NY:1981), p. 86.

[5] Tan, #4219

[6] Ibid., #3534.

[7] Johnson, p. 114.

Chapter 7

[1] Tan, #1974.

[2] Ibid., #4577.

[3] Ibid., #4532.

[4] Cowman, September 20.

[5] Dutton, Dean, *Quests and Conquests,* (Life Service Publishing Co., Guthrie, OK: 1923), # 161.

[6] Tan, #4578.

Chapter 8

[1] Tan, #4567.

Chapter 9

[1] Tan, #4567.

[2] Wallace, pp163-166.

[3] DeMoss, p. 136.

[4] Dutton, #1592.

Chapter 10

[1] Ravenhill, p. 156.

OTHER BOOKS BY JOY HANEY

<u>PAPERBACK</u>
The Radiant Woman
The Seven Parchments
Those Bloomin' Kids
Pressed Down But Looking Up
The Privilege Woman
Great Faith
Phillip's Family
The Elite
The Dreamers
What Do You Do When You Don't Feel Like Doing What You're Doing?
The Blessing of the Trial
Cuando Ayuneis
Modern Day Abraham
How to have Radiant Health
The Healing Power of Prayer
Nothing But the Best: A Call to Excellence
How to Forgive When It's Hard to Forget
The Magical Gift of Kindness
Diamonds for Dusty Roads
How to have a Wonderful Marriage
Kenneth F. Haney: A Man With a Vision
When Ye Pray
When Ye Fast
When Ye Give
At the Master's Feet, Volume I

continued on next page. . .

May I Wash Your Feet
The Carpenter
Behold the Nazarite Woman
Women of the Spirit Bible Studies:

Vol. I:	*Love God's Way*
Vol. II:	*Faith, Prayer & Spiritual Warfare*
Vol. III:	*All About Trials*
Vol. IV:	*Wisdom, Attitudes & Character*
Vol. V:	*Women of Compassion*
Vol. VI:	*The Power of Praise*
Vol. VII:	*JOY*

HARDBACK
His Angels
A Woman's Cry for Love
(a Full-color gift book of English & Italian Sonnets)

CASSETTES AND CD'S
Clean Out the Ashes on Cassette (book on tape)
Pray in the Spirit (singing tape & CD)